P9-BZH-360

HOW TO GRADE
U.S. COINS

*A Step-by-step guide
to the grading of
uncirculated and proof coins.*

by James L. Halperin

A Publication by Ivy Press, Inc.
Heritage Plaza • Highland Park Village • Dallas, Texas 75205-2788

Copyright © 1990 by Ivy Press, Inc.

All rights reserved.

Reproduction or translation of any part of this work without
permission of the copyright owner is unlawful. Requests for
permission or further information should be addressed to
       Ivy Press, Inc.
       Heritage Plaza
       Highland Park Village
       Dallas, Texas 75205-2788

Library of Congress Catalog No.: 86-82031
ISBN: 0-933372-02-7

Printed in the United States of America

Cover photo by ©Elle Schuster, 1990

Notice

The grading standards described in this book are not the only ones in use today. They are not necessarily the "correct" standards, because, in my opinion, there are no "correct" standards. I don't mean to assign any particular value to coins graded by these standards. There is presently a great deal of controversy surrounding the "true" definition of MINT STATE-65 and PROOF-65 as well as other mint state coin grades.

The standards outlined in this book are the approximate ones currently (as of June, 1990) employed by the Professional Coin Grading Service (P.C.G.S.) and the Numismatic Guaranty Corporation of America (N.G.C.). They represent what I believe are the most accepted standards on today's market. They should not be confused with the more technical standards currently employed by the American Numismatic Association Certification Service (A.N.A.C.S.) or the more liberal standard currently employed by the Numismatic Certification Institute (N.C.I.).

In the words of noted numismatist and former American Numismatic Association president, Q. David Bowers, "The interpretation of published grading standards is a moving target. The A.N.A. grading service itself has changed its interpretations for many coins over the years." Thus, grading standards are constantly changing as the nature of the coin market changes.

Grading is fundamentally subjective, and the methods used to set a grade still often vary from dealer to dealer and from grading service to grading service. And the grading services themselves will sometimes grade a coin differently when it is submitted more than once. However, the methods outlined in this book are the product of a great deal of research. I have discussed even the most trivial components of grading with many dealers, particularly those recognized as the most competent wholesale coin traders. Great effort has been made to reach as objective a consensus as possible. Even so, some will certainly disagree with these conclusions. One of the goals of this book is to help improve consistency within the numismatic industry. However, total agreement throughout this industry will never come about because human subjectivity will always be a factor. Only the market itself can be the final arbiter of what ultimately determines the "true" grade of a coin (if there is such as thing as the "true" grade).

©Copyright 1990, James L. Halperin. All rights reserved.

Table of Contents

ACKNOWLEDGEMENTS

Even though this book carries my name as author, it has really been the product of much time and effort from many individuals. The idea of publishing a grading guide for uncirculated and proof coins was originally conceived by my partner, Steve Ivy.

Numismatic ideas and suggestions, as well as some sorely needed editorial help were selflessly provided by the following numismatic luminaries:

John Albanese	Greg Lauderdale
Buddy Alleva	Kevin Lipton
Bruce Amspacher	Ed Milas
Q. David Bowers	Lee Minshull
David Dekraker	Paul Nuggett
John Dannreuther	Martin Paul
Silvano DiGenova	William Paul
Marc Emory	Greg Roberts
Bill Fivaz	Maurice Rosen
David Ganz	Greg Rohan
Ronald Guth	Michael Sherman
David Hall	Harvey Stack
Ron Howard	Paul Taglione
Steve Ivy	Scott Travers
John Kamin	Mark Van Winkle

Some of the coins photographed herein were loaned to us by: Charles Anastasio, Jack Beymer, Donald Brigandi, John Dannreuther, Ed Hipps, Larry Whitlow, Rick Montgomery (A.N.A.C.S.), Jeff Garrett, and Harlan White.

Greg Rohan conceived and practically wrote the chapter entitled "Why Won't They Grade My Coin?" The chapter entitled "Computer Grading" **was** written by David Dekraker. I barely even had to edit it.

In addition, my sister, Marjorie Halperin and my mother, Audrey Halperin, did an outstanding job editing the text.

Michael Haynes, Michael Sherman, Blaine Leist, Clarke Blacker, James Duke, Missy Robbins, Marsha Cathey, Jody Garver, Budd Perlman, Cathy Anstedt-Hadd, Rod Downey, Carl Watson and the rest of the staff of Heritage's Marketing department are responsible for the beautiful photography and graphics.

Finally, this entire project would have been virtually impossible without the tireless effort of my brilliant secretary and administrative assistant, Judy Davidson.

James L. Halperin

Introduction

By Scott A. Travers
Copyright ©1990 Scott A. Travers

Imagine yourself trying to assemble the pieces of a huge jigsaw puzzle of a map of a land foreign to you. You could try to find the four corners; then proceed from there. Or you could spread out sections of matching parts across the living-room floor and go through the rest of the puzzle's pieces, hoping to find some part – any part! – that would fit neatly into the assemblage.

The puzzle would be difficult to solve if you didn't have any idea of what it should look like put together: your best guesses as to which piece goes where might be hopelessly **wrong.** Think what it would be like trying to assemble that jigsaw puzzle if some of the pieces were missing! Imagine how you would feel if you found out that whole sections of fitting pieces didn't pertain to the puzzle you were assembling! Try grading an uncirculated coin!

For the newcomer, the process of grading coins can be likened to a jigsaw puzzle. No one book holds all the pieces to the puzzle. Rather, each participant in the marketplace holds his or her own secret, magical piece. But James L. Halperin holds an incredible number of those valuable pieces. In this book, he is willing to boldly share with you his opinions and grading insights (" . . . no guts, no glory!").

How to Grade U.S. Coins is an important and necessary piece required to solve the great grading puzzle. Before this book was published, if you were looking for a grading **standard**, you had a choice of three books, each one of which was – and still is – a necessary piece of the puzzle: *A Guide to the Grading of U.S. Coins*, by Martin R. Brown and John W. Dunn (Western Publishing, Inc. 1958); *Photograde*, by James F. Ruddy (Bowers & Merena Galleries, Inc., 1972); and *Official A.N.A. Grading Standards for United States Coins*, by the American Numismatic Association (Western Publishing, Inc., 1981). *How to Grade U.S. Coins* (Ivy Press, 1990) has to be added to this list.

If you're comparing books which consist of **only** grading standards, you'll probably reach the conclusion that, as of this writing, this book is the best for the grading of Mint State coins. It's the **only** grading standards book which defines a precise formulated standard for the grading of Mint State coins.

The 7th edition of the Brown and Dunn work doesn't recognize that there are differences among Mint State coins: Only "Uncirculated" is recognized. Ruddy's work is substantial and important if you're grading **circulated** coins. But there are no standards for Mint State. And although the A.N.A.'s grading guide has line drawings for every major United States coin type, the standards for grading Mint State coins are not clearly defined. In a public statement, the A.N.A. admitted that "The grading standards enumerated in (its) book were and are not precise, with the descriptions lending themselves to different interpretations."

In this book Jim Halperin is straightforward. He tells you that N.C.I. is not as conservative as A.N.A.C.S. Jim admits to making money (six-figures on one coin **after** he dipped it). He conceedes that you might be able to find N.C.I. certified coins at considerably below what a price guide might indicate for that grade. And he makes clear that *The N.C.I. Grading Guide*, the predecessor to this book, defined only The Numismatic Certification Institute's own standards.

A great professor could write a persuasive work on the grading of coins. He could use a formula similar to Jim Halperin's. But the professor would only be able to express theoretical concepts. The fact that this book was written by someone with the awesome real-world experience that Jim has is testimony to the significance of **this** book.

Jim Halperin invented "spot" decision-making when he headed New England Rare Coin Galleries in the 1970's. If a multi-thousand dollar deal was offered to him at a specific price, he'd accept, decline, or counter-offer in a matter of seconds. If he made a mistake, he'd live with it and go on to the next deal. Although quick dealing had always been part of the coin industry, Jim institutionalized the practice. An he did it just in time for the coin boom of 1979-1980. You'd go to a coin convention during that boom, and there were dealers trying to emulate Halperin: no magnifying glass; a quick glance at the coins; and an offer.

Jim hired a large number of numismatists, many of whom quickly picked up spot decision making. Most of them now have their own successful companies. A staggering percentage of today's most successful coin dealers have worked for Jim at one time or another.

I remember a coin convention in early 1981. I was sitting and discussing coin grading with David Hall, not yet the founder of P.C.G.S., but even then one of America's leading dealers. Jim Halperin walked by briskly, on his way to price a deal; or sell a coin; or buy a coin; but, in any event, to act quickly. "Don't you ever wonder what it must be like to be the best person in the entire world at pricing coins?" Hall asked, referring to Halperin. "The man is just amazing!" he exclaimed, displaying his characteristic enthusiasm over someone or something he believes in. "At least right now, there is nobody who is his equal at quick pricing and knowing values," he continued. "It must be just an incredible feeling to know that you're at the top of your industry and the best in the entire world at doing something."

Despite any criticism that anyone might ever have about Jim Halperin, or his spot decision making, the fact remains that the man helped to revolutionize the way coins are bought and sold; and he has phenomenal experience at grading coins.

So as you ponder the complexities of coin grading and try to solve the great grading puzzle, remember to give this book your most serious consideration. *The Rare Coin Grading Guide* might well be the single missing piece that you've been looking for.

Scott A. Travers is author of *Rare Coin Investment Strategy* and *The Coin Collector's Survival Manual*, the Numismatic Literary Guild's 1985 "Book of the Year." Mr. Travers is an award-winning contributor to numismatic publications and contributing editor at *COINage* magazine. He is a frequent speaker on television and radio talk shows. Mr. Travers holds a B.A. from Brandeis University.

Preface

"Science seeks generally only the most useful systems of classification: these it regards (as true) for the time being, until more useful classifications are invented as true." – S.I. Hayakawa

It is doubtful that the science of rare coin grading has ever changed so dramatically as it has in the past twenty years. Since the early 1970's, numismatics has been transformed from almost a pure hobby to a fairly sophisticated investment medium. Those of us just starting in the rare coin business (I opened my first rare coin store in 1968) could see that a change was coming. It was obvious that investors would soon be invading the hobby. However, none of us had any idea of the impact that the rare coin investment business and the new technologies adapted to deal with it, were about to have on the entire field of numismatics.

Since the early days of coin collecting, numismatists have needed a method to describe the quality of a particular coin. However, until recent times coin grading was informal at best. One coin collector would simply try to get accustomed to the meaning of the terms of description employed by each dealer he knew. After enough dealings with that dealer, he would usually know from the description whether or not that coin was suitable for his collection.

There have been many attempts to standardize grading throughout history. The American Numismatic Association actually had a grading committee from 1908 to 1911. Numerous attempts were made to set standards for a particular series, such as the Gettys-Catich articles on grading commemorative half dollars, which appeared in *"The Numismatist."* However, one would have to say that the first effective effort was authored by Martin R. Brown and John W. Dunn in 1958. As far as I know, *A Guide to the Grading of United States Coins*, was the first illustrated, scientific guide to the grading of United States coins. In 1970 James F. Ruddy (See footnote #1) authored an even more useful grading guide entitled *Photograde*. As a result of these two important works, the grading of circulated United States coins has remained relatively standard and uncontroversial for the last two or three decades.

Since 1970, however, the grading of circulated coins has become a far less important part of the total grading picture. On the whole, investors seek the highest quality coins available. This drives up the prices of those coins. As more investors enter the market, a much larger segment of the total value of the market comes to be composed of the highest quality (i.e. uncirculated and proof) coinage.

Many of those familiar with the Sheldon grading system (Numbers 1 through 70) will be surprised to learn that Dr. Sheldon's system was originally designed to apply only to copper coinage. Mint state grading (MS-60, 65 and 70) applied mostly to color. A brown uncirculated coin was MS-60, a red and brown coin was MS-65, and a full red large cent was MS-70. Bagmarks, strike, lustre and eye-appeal were far less crucial to the grade.

Even more interesting was Dr. Sheldon's attempt to relate grade to value. When he devised his system in the late 1940's, it was his intention that anyone would be able to assign a value to any grade of a particular coin merely by multiplying its base or "basal" value by the numerical grade. (The Sheldon system did provide an additional premium if a coin was among the finest of its kind. However, this wouldn't make a significant difference when dealing with common varieties). Thus, a Mint State-70 coin would, in theory, have been priced at exactly three and one half times the price of a VERY FINE-20 coin. Of course this system seems particularly bizarre in light of today's pricing structure. Now a MINT STATE-65 example of a common date large cent might bring over a hundred times the price of a VERY FINE coin.

Actually, the Sheldon system did not gain any acceptance outside of the large cent collectors' community until the early 1970's. When the system was first introduced to Morgan and Peace silver dollars, the intention was for MS-60 to refer to a mint state coin with normal to heavy bagmarks. MS-65 described an above average mint state coin with fewer than normal bagmarks, and an MS-70 was an exceptional uncirculated coin, which might fall somewhere close to today's MS-65 grade. In fact, I remember Paramount International Coin Corporation (see footnote #2), at that time one of America's largest and most respected dealers in U.S. coins, running several full page *Coin World* and *Numismatic News* advertisements using the Sheldon scale. These ads listed EVERY DATE of Morgan and Peace Dollars in MINT STATE-65, and the vast majority of dates in MINT STATE-70 grade.

To put things into better perspective: in fewer than 15 years, a MINT STATE-65 coin has gone from being an above average mint state coin (approximately 1 out of 2 or 3) to being a choice or gem coin (perhaps 1 out of 25!). The reason for this change is that there has never been a standard for grading mint state coins. If the pricing guides said that a MINT STATE-65 Barber Quarter was worth $3,000, then a Barber Quarter worth $3,000 was "today's" Mint State-65. That didn't mean the same coin would be tomorrow's MINT STATE-65, when the pricing guides say $5,000, nor did it mean that coin was last year's MINT STATE-65, when the pricing guides listed MS-65 Barber Quarters at $2,000.

The dealers set their grading standards for mint state coins based on the pricing guides. And the pricing guides didn't have to be reliable or meaningful in their own right; the grading standards themselves would change to accommodate the prices reported. It was even more difficult to tell the difference between grading changes, incompetence, and outright dishonesty. Suppose you bought a coin as MS-65 in 1978, and could only sell it for an MS-60+ price in 1984. Was it because the standards had changed, or because of a bad buy? The answer is by no means clear. It was a confusing system for dealers, and it must have been totally baffling to a novice collector or investor.

In 1984, my partner, Steve Ivy and I set up the Numismatic Certification Institute (N.C.I.) in an attempt to standardize grading. Our goal was for coins graded by N.C.I. to be considered consistently graded enough to trade sight-unseen by dealers. The concept worked very well, and became part of the inspiration for an even better concept, P.C.G.S.

In 1986, David Hall, who will probably be remembered as the greatest numismatic marketing genius of this century (probably even more than B. Max Mehl) founded P.C.G.S. The P.C.G.S. concept was to grade coins by the consensus of a panel of experts, and then seal these coins in tamper-proof plastic holders. David Hall put together a group of America's leading dealers to trade in P.C.G.S. graded coins on a sight-unseen basis. Today, P.C.G.S. coins trade over a national electronic trading network. As of this writing P.C.G.S. has graded literally millions of coins with a total market value well into ten figures!

In 1987, N.G.C. entered the market using a similar grading standard. Both services are highly respected, and have made a major contribution to the efficiency of trading in the rare coin market.

But perhaps even more important is the contribution these two superb services have made to numismatic education, albeit inadvertently. Now a collector, investor or dealer can view hundreds or even thousands of coins at a single coin convention or auction, all graded by essentially the same standard. What a great way to practice and learn coin grading skills! As a direct result of P.C.G.S. and N.G.C. (and I like to think to some extent, N.C.I.) it is much easier today to become a skilled grader of uncirculated and proof coins than it has ever been in the past.

Grading *circulated* coins has never been especially difficult. Practically anyone can learn how to do it with practice and study. Grading circulated coins is a "piece of cake" compared to grading mint state coins. The following humorous story makes a good analogy.

Imagine a Martian spaceship hovering above a golf course. Two Martians observe an Earthling slice his first shot into the rough. His second shot lands in a sandtrap. His third shot rolls well past the green. And so on. Finally, his eleventh shot is a heroic chip onto the green, which miraculously rolls into the hole. The first Martian turns to the other and says, "Looks like he's really in trouble now."

Most coin investors are just like the Martian. Not only do they have no idea how to grade mint state and proof coins . . . they don't even know the basic rules of the game. So first things first. In this guide, I am going to try to teach you the basic rules of grading. Then I'm going to describe some of the finer points. But first, I'm going to suggest to you a few ideas on ways to gain sufficient practice in order to make a respectable showing at the game of coin grading itself.

"Never learn to do anything; if you don't learn, you'll always find someone else to do it for you." – Mark Twain

The preceding advice was sarcastic. Mark Twain was poking fun at human laziness, which often causes us to depend on other people's judgement. Nobody can be depended on to look after our own interests as well as we would ourselves. Yet we've all been guilty of that sort of laziness at some time in our lives.

The next obvious question is: What if I don't have time to learn coin grading? The answer is that if you don't learn how to grade, then you will lose a certain edge in your coin purchasing efforts. You might still find coins to be a very profitable investment, just as a very knowledgeable investor can still lose money due to bad timing or bad luck. However, the more time you are willing to devote to your education, the more successful you are likely to be. No matter how competent and honest your coin dealer is, he is not going to be able to help you maximize value for your money the way you could yourself if you knew how to grade coins. Grading is at least partially subjective. Every dealer has purchased and sold both undergraded and overgraded coins. Even if you buy only certified coins, you are better off knowing how to grade coins. How else can you tell whether or not a coin is really PQ (Premium Quality) for the grade? Let's face facts. It is human nature for a dealer to give his own coin the "benefit of the doubt." Sure, you could get lucky and buy a coin that's been slightly undergraded. But that's going to happen less often than the other way around. The best coins are the ones that are most likely to sell before you ever have a chance to buy them.

Don't be discouraged if you don't think you can ever become an expert. Nobody alive knows everything there is to know about coin grading (or golf, or practically anything else). Just remember: In the long run, the more you know the better you are likely to do financially with coins.

Read this book carefully. Start by reading the GLOSSARY. You will probably find it helpful to refer to the GLOSSARY as you read the rest of this book. Then you will have, as your basic foundation, a fundamental understanding of how grading works. After this is accomplished, the best way to continue and **really** learn how to grade is to attend an auction or a coin show and look at a LOT of coins.

Now for those of you who are ready to jump in and begin to learn, let me offer you some final advice: don't be a know-it-all! No matter how many times you read this book, you still won't know one tenth as much as most dealers who have gone to numerous coin shows and auctions, and have spent entire days at a time just looking at coins. Until you really know coins, don't contradict anything that a dealer tells you, or volunteer an opinion. You can't possibly learn everything you need to know about grading from any book. There's plenty of information that isn't in this book which *could* explain why that dealer's coin might be MS-65 even though you're positive it's only MS-63 (or AU-55). If you have any doubts, you're perfectly within your rights not to buy the coin. The best part is that you're not expected to give a reason.

Also, if you spend a few hours looking through a firm's auction lots, or take 20 minutes of a dealer's time while he shows you coins, you should feel some obligation to at least **try** to buy something. If possible, find something relatively inexpensive that you happen to like. It is only fair. And you'll learn something about how that dealer does business as well.

The best place to look at a lot of coins with a minimum of hassle is at a major rare coin auction. You can easily look at hundreds of mint state and proof coins in a single sitting. Purchase a copy of the catalog and compare the coins to the descriptions. Test how you tend to grade the coins in relation to the cataloger. Pay particular attention to the P.C.G.S. and N.G.C. graded coins, as these will nearly always be the most consistently graded. If you think a coin is vastly overgraded or undergraded, make a discreet note in your catalog. Then see what price the coin brings. Does the market agree or disagree with you? (There are numerous reasons why the auction price realized may not, in some cases, be a fair representation of the market. Still, this exercise will be a very useful part of your learning process).

Always try to look at coins under similar conditions. This is especially true with regard to lighting and magnification. For example, I always try to look at coins under a 100 watt incandescent lightbulb. However, a 60 or 75 watt bulb, or a tensor lamp is also perfectly acceptable, so long as you always use the same type light and intensity. I prefer approximately a 5X magnifying glass when looking at proof coins or coins smaller than a dime, and no magnification for anything else. I suppose you can get accustomed to any kind of magnification, but I feel that too much magnification is confusing.

In most cases, the coins you look at will either be in P.C.G.S. or N.G.C. holders or be contained in some sort of plastic "flips." It isn't reasonable to expect a dealer or auctioneer to remove the coins from these flips, as the coins can easily become damaged through mishandling. Sometimes the plastic will develop hairlines, and I find that a 5X magnifying glass is very useful for determining whether the hairlines are on the plastic or on the coin. If you still can't tell, gently move the coin within the flip to distinguish whether hairlines, spots, etc. belong to the flip or to the coin itself.

If you are given the opportunity to look at a group of coins outside of their flips (or when you're studying your own coins), be sure to handle them very carefully, BY THE EDGES ONLY. At no time should your fingers ever touch the obverse or reverse surfaces of a coin. Always view your coins over a soft surface such as a felt pad or towel. That way, if you should ever drop a coin, it probably won't be damaged.

Finally, the best way to see how well you're doing at mastering grading is to actually send some of your purchases to the P.C.G.S. or N.G.C. grading services. Compare your opinion to theirs. I realize that there are other competent grading services. However, since the standards you are about to learn from this book are the P.C.G.S. and N.G.C. standards, it is best, for the sake of consistency, that you use P.C.G.S. and N.G.C. for this purpose. It is hoped that as you gain experience, your grading will *tend* to coincide with theirs. Once you find yourself in agreement with them 85-90% of the time (that's approximately their own consistency rate; i.e. the percentage of the time they grade each coin the same, since no one is 100% consistent), you won't need this book any more!

"Money can't buy happiness, but it can buy you the kind of misery you prefer." – Author unkown

Even with today's expanded numerical system, there are only 11 mint state grades (60, 61, 62, 63, 64, 65, 66, 67, 68, 69 and 70). Yet if you had 1,000 or more of the same coin, all in uncirculated condition, it would be theoretically possible to rank them in order from best to worst. Therefore some MS-63's for example are going to be just barely MS-63, while others may be very close to MS-64. Naturally, the latter coins may command a significant premium over the former.

The trick now is to be able to distinguish a premium quality coin from a low-end coin.

It can be very helpful to know how to grade so that you can tell when a correctly graded coin is at the higher or lower end of that grade. As I have stated previously, you can never learn it all. But clearly, the more you know about grading, the better off you are. This is the real value of the third party grading opinion and of your own knowledge. Both are subjective, and certainly nowhere near foolproof. However, both can be important tools that can help improve your chances of success.

"Don't hurry, don't worry. You're only here for a short visit. So be sure to stop and smell the flowers." – From the New York Times, 5/22/77

One last bit of wisdom; As long as you're going to this much trouble, please don't forget to enjoy coins. Not only will enjoyment make the learning easier, but it also should become an end in itself. People collect because coins are interesting and fun! The best way to understand the collector mentality is to become a collector yourself. Even if you don't make a profit, at least you will have received something for your trouble. It's a funny thing though. As you learn more about coins, and start to buy the coins that appeal most to you, your judgments will start to coincide with the future of the coin market. Collectors often seem to be one step ahead of the investors. They usually have a better instinct for value. Collectors are the underlying basis of the coin market, a fact of which investors so often lose sight. To improve their chances of success, investors should try to predict which coins will be the most sought after by **collectors** ten or twenty years from now. Therefore, it really isn't so surprising that the most committed, passionate collectors often realize a better financial return when they sell their coins than many serious investors do.

©Copyright 1990, James L. Halperin. All rights reserved.

GLOSSARY

Adjustment Marks – Scratches which appear mostly on pre-1807 silver and gold coinage. These scratches were file marks, made at the mint in order to reduce the weight of a coin so that its metal value wouldn't exceed its face value. As such, adjustment marks do not reduce the value of a coin nearly as much as a series of equally visible scratches which were not "mint-caused."

A.N.A. – Abbreviation for the American Numismatic Association. The A.N.A. is the world's largest organization of coin collectors and dealers. It is a non-profit organization, chartered by an Act of Congress in 1912. Membership is highly recommended. If you are not a member, you should be! See membership application at the end of this book. Address: 818 N. Cascade Ave., Colorado Springs, Colorado, 80901.

A.N.E. – Abbreviation for American Numismatic Information Exchange. P.C.G.S. and N.G.C. certified coins trade sight-unseen through this electronic network.

A.N.A.C.S. – Abbreviation for American Numismatic Association Certification Service. A.N.A.C.S. is a service which grades and authenticates coins. A.N.A.C.S. grading tends to be somewhat technical, and is often a bit more conservative than P.C.G.S. or N.G.C. grading. A.N.A.C.S. has recently been acquired by Amos Press, the publisher of *Coin World.*

Ask – The lowest asking price of a particular coin offered for sale by one dealer to another as reported by the *Coin Dealer Newsletter.* The "ask" price is usually about 10% higher than the "bid" price. (See "Bid").

Bagmarks – Abrasions which occur on coins that were shipped in mint bags. Most often this term applies to silver dollars, although virtually any coin can have bagmarks. Bagmarks in no way mean that a coin is not mint state. In fact, even a Mint State-67 coin can have *some* bagmarks.

Bid – The highest price offered to buy a particular coin by one dealer from other dealers, as reported by the *Coin Dealer Newsletter.* When applied to circulated coins, and other fairly standard items, the bid/ask prices are usually accurate, meaningful and useful. When applied to mint state coins, especially Mint State and Proof 65, they can be somewhat misleading. The implication is that all MS-65's are equal, which is simply not the case. In fact, no two coins are absolutely identical. One buyer's MS-65 is often another buyer's MS-64+ or MS-65+. The CDN "Bid" prices generally reflect wholesale trading ranges for only the most conservatively graded mint state coins. Sight-unseen bid prices for P.C.G.S. coins are also listed on the A.N.E. network, and in the *Certified Coin Dealer Newsletter.* Of course, sight-unseen bids are almost always lower than sight-seen prices such as dealer-to-dealer transactions at coin shows. (See "A.N.E." and "C.C.D.N.")

Brilliant – Untoned. Without tarnish or oxidation, and with original cartwheel (i.e. frosty) or prooflike lustre. A copper coin is usually referred to as brilliant if it has full original red. A silver, nickel or gold coin is usually descibed as brilliant if it has no toning or oxidation (although it may have some spots or light toning hues about the periphery), and its original lustre is more or less intact.

Brilliant Proof – A particular type of proof coin, which boasts a full mirror surface in the fields. (See "Proof," "Matte Proof," and "Roman Finish.")

Business Strike – A coin which was struck for use in general circulation, as opposed to a proof coin produced strictly for collector purposes.

Cameo – A proof, or prooflike coin with exceptional contrast between the fields and the devices. On a cameo coin, the fields are mirrorlike, while the devices give a frosty appearance.

Carbon Spot – A dark discoloration on the surface of a coin. It is possible that this discoloration is caused by a planchet imperfection prior to striking, or it may be caused by improper storage of the coin. Regardless of the cause, carbon spots are difficult, if not impossible, to remove without leaving pits in the coin's surface. If they are large enough, they can significantly lower the grade and value of a coin.

Cartwheel – An effect caused by the natural lustre on most mint state, and on some proof coins. When the coin is tilted back and forth, beams of light seem to circle the central devices of the coin.

C.C.D.N. – Abbreviation for *Certified Coin Dealer Newsletter.* A weekly newsletter which as of today (June, 1990) lists sight-unseen bid prices for coins certified by P.C.G.S., N.G.C., A.N.A.C.S. and N.C.I. Probably the best source of pricing information available to the coin collector or investor. However; the prices listed tend to be on the low side, since the bids are sight-unseen. Address: P.O. Box 11099, Torrance, California. Subscription rate: $99 per year. (See "Bid.")

Choice – An adjective which the A.N.A. applies to coins of MS-65 or Proof-65 grade. Many dealers apply the term to MS/Proof-63 coins, and call MS/Proof-65 coins "Gem."

Cleaned – When a coin has been cleaned with baking soda or other mild abrasives, it may take on a slightly washed out look. Most dealers can tell that the coin has been cleaned. For all practical purposes, however, it is impossible to tell if most silver or gold coins have been judiciously and expertly cleaned just once or twice in Jewel-Lustre(c) or soap and water, or any other basically non-abrasive solution. If the lustre or color of the coin appears even the slightest bit unnatural as a result of past cleaning, the coin is usually described as "cleaned" when catalogued for sale.

Coin Dealer Newsletter – A weekly newsletter that reports the trading ranges of nearly all U.S. coins. Grading differences can cause the reported prices to be somewhat confusing at times. Address: P.O. Box 11099, Torrance, California, 90510. Subscription rate: $89 per year.

Coin World – A leading weekly coin publication. Published by Amos Press, P. O. Box 150, Sidney, Ohio, 45365. Subscription rate: 52 weeks for $23.95.

Commercial Grade – A synonym for Market Grade.

Conservative Grade – A grade which gives the "benefit of the doubt" to the purchaser rather than to the seller.

Corrosion – Damage which occurs on the surface of some coins, generally due to improper storage. Corrosion is caused when a chemical reaction, such as rust, actually eats into the metal.

Clashed Dies – Extraneous design detail often appears on a die as a result of two dies coming together without a planchet between them during the minting process. Coins struck from such dies are said to be struck from clashed dies, or to have die clashes or clash marks. (See "Die," "Die Scratches.")

Denticles – The toothlike projections which make up the inner rim on some coins. They were discontinued on most United States coins in the early twentieth century.

Devices – The focal figure(s) of a coin, such as Miss Liberty's head and the eagle which appear on the Morgan silver dollar.

Die – The metal mold used to strike a coin.

Die Cracks – Raised lines which appear on a coin as a result of that coin having been struck by a cracked die.

Die Rust – Pitting or roughness appearing on a coin as a result of that coin having been struck by a rusted die.

Die Scratches – Raised lines which appear on a coin as a result of scratches on the die used to strike that coin. Die scratches (and similarly die cracks and die clashes) do not diminish the value of a coin nearly as much as scratches acquired after the coin is struck. In many cases, they do not affect the value of the coin at all.

Die Variety – A coin which has already been attributed by denomination, date, mintmark and major variety (such as Morgan Dollar, 1879-S, Reverse of '78) can often still be broken down by die variety. Research has been done in many series assigning numbers to the various combinations of dies known to have struck coins of each of the various years and mintmarks. A few examples of reference works on die varieties are: Sheldon (large cents), Valentine (half dimes), Browning (early quarters), Overton (bust half dollars), Van-Allen/Mallis (Morgan silver dollars), and Breen (U.S. gold coins $1 through $10).

Die Wear – The loss of detail on a coin due to wear on the die used to strike it (rather than wear on the coin itself).

D.M.P.L. – Abbreviation for Deep Mirror Prooflike. An exceptionally deep mirror-like prooflike coin with little if any cartwheel lustre. Synonym: "D.P.L." (See P.L.)

Dipped – A coin which has been cleaned in a soap solution, the most popular of which is called "Jewel Luster"(c), is said to have been dipped. The term "dipped" is not considered necessary in, say, a catalog description of a coin, unless the dipping has caused noticeable dulling of lustre, or an otherwise unnatural appearance (usually on copper coins). The practice of dipping coins is not advisable, except by bonafide experts, and even then only on rare occasions.

Eye-Appeal – The aesthetic effect a coin has on its viewer. Although somewhat subjective, like any form of art, that which constitutes eye-appeal (or the lack of it) is generally agreed upon by most experienced numismatists.

Field – The flat part of a coin's surface which surrounds the devices, date, legend and other parts of the coin's design.

Flip – A clear, flexible plastic holder used to display and store coins. (See "PVC").

Friction – A disturbance which appears either on the high-points of a coin or in the fields, as a result of that coin rubbing against other objects. A coin is said to have friction when only the lustre is disturbed, and no actual wear of the metal is visible to the naked eye. Many strictly uncirculated coins can have some friction, often from storage in old style coin cabinets or albums or from rubbing against other coins in rolls. (See "Rubbing").

Frosty – An adjective used to describe a coin which possesses cartwheel lustre. (See "Cartwheel").

Gem – An adjective which the A.N.A. applies to coins which grade Mint State or Proof-67. Many dealers, however, apply the adjective to any coin which they grade MS/Proof-65.

Grey Sheet – A synonym for the Coin Dealer Newsletter.

Hairline – A thin, shallow scratch on the surface of a coin, usually caused by improper cleaning, or mishandling. Hairlines are found on virtually all proof coins, and are considered the most important single factor in grading high quality proof coins. They sometimes appear on business strikes as well. Hairlines tend to show up more often on prooflike business strikes.

Hallmark – An independent grading service in Woburn, Massachusetts recently formed by Q. David Bowers and Lee Bellisario.

High Relief – A coin with deep concave fields, due to its design. High relief coins required extra pressure to be fully struck, and were difficult to stack. Therefore, the few coins struck in high relief by the U.S. mint (such as the 1921 Peace dollar, and the 1907 Roman Numerals double eagle) were each made for only one year.

Iridescent – Probably the most desirable form of toning on a silver or nickel coin. Iridescent toning covers virtually all of the coin's surface, while still permitting all of the coin's natural lustre to shine through with its full intensity. Some numismatists feel that in order for toning to be called iridescent it must have all the colors of the rainbow, or at the very least, most of them.

Lamination – A form of planchet flaw caused by imperfections in the metal, whereby a thin strip of the metal separates itself from the coin.

Lint Mark – A characteristic which occurs mostly on proof coins as a result of a piece of lint on the die or planchet during the striking process. This lint creates an incused scratch-like mark on the coin. Lint marks are distinguishable from hairlines by their evenness of depth and lack of raised ridges on their borders. They are also identifiable by their interesting thread-like shapes. Since a lint-mark is mint caused, it has a much smaller effect on the grade and value of a coin, than a hairline of equal size and prominence.

Lustre – The brightness of a coin which results from the way in which it reflects light. Many different types of lustre exist, and one of the trickiest parts of the grading process is determining whether the lustre of a coin is artificial (See "whizzed"), natural as made, or diminshed through wear, cleaning, friction, temperature, humidity, etc. (Alternate spelling "Luster.")

Market Grade – The grade at which most reputable dealers and auction houses would offer an uncertified coin. Also the standard employed by the N.C.I. (Numismatic Certification Institute) grading service. Often the retail market grade is less conservative than the technical grade. Factors other than the state of preservation are taken into account. Generally, a coin graded by retail market standards trades dealer to dealer at less than the current *Coin Dealer Newsletter* "bid" price, but often substantially over the "bid" price for the next lowest grade. CDN "bid" prices usually reflect wholesale trading ranges for the most conservatively graded coins on the market. (Synonym: "Commercial Grade").

Matte Proof – A certain type of proof minted in the U.S. mostly from 1908 to 1916. Gold and silver matte proofs have a dull, granular (i.e. sandblast) finish without any mirror-like qualities. Copper and nickel matte proofs are really more like Roman finish proofs. (See "Roman Finish").

Milling Mark – A series of two or more small nicks on a coin which result from contact with the reeded edge of another coin, usually in a mint bag. Milling marks are generally more detrimental to the grade than normal bagmarks, because of their severity of depth and greater visual impact. (Synonym: "Reeding Mark").

Mint State – Describes a coin which has never been circulated. Thus, the coin has no wear. A mint state coin may still be weakly struck, and therefore lack the detail of even a lower grade coin. All mint state coins have some imperfections if you study them hard enough. The term "mint state" may also correctly be applied to coins that were struck as proofs.

Mishandled Proof – A proof coin which somehow escaped into circulation or was otherwise significantly abused.

N.C.I. – Abbreviation for Numismatic Certification Institute, Dallas, Texas.

N.G.C. – Abbreviation for Numismatic Guaranty Corporation of America, Parsippany, New Jersey. A leading independent grading service.

Numismatic News – A leading weekly coin newspaper. Published by Krause Publications, 700 E. State St., Iola, Wisc. 54990. Subscription rate: 52 weeks for $23.00.

Obverse – The front, or "heads" side of a coin. Usually the side with the date.

Original – Referring to any aspect of a coin that retains its original state. Original toning means natural, not retoned or cleaned. Original lustre means undisturbed lustre that hasn't been enhanced through artificial means.

Original Roll – A roll of coins, all the same date, denomination, and mint mark, and usually of the same die variety, which seem to have been acquired by the same original owner, probably from the same original mint bag. Generally, all the coins in an original roll will have similar toning and lustre.

P.C.G.S. – Abbreviation for Professional Coin Grading Service, Irvine, California. Currently the leading independent grading service.

Patina – See "Toning."

P.L. – Abbreviation for Prooflike. A coin struck for general circulation which has, nonetheless, a somewhat mirror-like surface, similar to a brilliant proof. Prooflike coins are usually among the first coins to have been struck from a newly polished die. Naturally, unlimited degrees of prooflikeness exist. (See "Cameo" and "Semi-Prooflike.")

Planchet – The blank metal disk which becomes a coin when struck under high pressure between two dies.

Planchet Defect – Any defect of a coin which was caused by the planchet being imperfect prior to the coin being struck. (Synonym: "Planchet Flaw").

PQ – An abbreviation devised by Q. David Bowers in November, 1985. It stands for "Premium Quality," a term which describes the very finest coins which fall into the categories of Mint State-65 or Proof-65. For example, an MS-65PQ graded coin is considered more desirable than a coin described simply as MS-65. It should be noted that, as of this writing, the term is not (yet) universally used in this context, although Hallmark grading service employs the term on some coins it grades.

Presentation Piece – A coin which was obviously given special care when being struck. Similar to a proof, but not necessarily formally struck as one.

Proof – A coin which was made with special care, exclusively for collectors or investors and not struck for general circulation. Generally, proof coins are struck on specially selected and polished planchets. They are struck using polished dies. Usually the coins are made on a slower moving press, and/or are struck more than once. Most proof coins are brilliant, with a mirror-like surface. (See "Matte Proof," "Roman Finish," "Brilliant Proof," and "Cameo"). Proof is a method of manufacture, not a grade. However, proof coins are generally graded using the Sheldon scale (for example; Proof-60 or Proof-65).

PVC – Poly-Vinyl Chloride, a somewhat active chemical found in some types of plastic coin flips. PVC will cause some coins to tone or turn green over time. The effect is negligible on silver or gold coins (and removable), but PVC has been known to wreak havoc on copper, and to a lesser extent nickel coins, especially if the coins have been stored in warm or damp places over long periods of time. (See "Flip").

Raw – Refers to any coin which has not been graded by a grading service.

Red & Brown – A term used to describe mint state (and sometimes proof) copper coins which have started to turn brown, but still show some of their original mint red.

Retoned – Coin dealer slang for a coin which has been artificially toned, usually through some sort of chemical means.

Reverse – The back or "tails" side of a coin.

Rip – Coin dealer slang for a coin which was purchased below the market wholesale price and is easily resalable to one or more coin dealers for a good profit.

Roman Finish – A hybrid between a brilliant proof surface and a matte surface. Roman finish proof gold coins were struck by the U.S. mint in 1909 and 1910, although a few examples exist in other years. Some consider Roman finish proofs to be the most beautiful of all proof coins. (Synonym: "Satin Finish").

Rubbing – The barest trace of wear on the high points of a coin. Just a step above "Friction" on the scale of adjectives used to describe degrees of wear. Usually, a coin with rubbing has virtually full mint lustre intact. Still, the wear is just a hair too noticeable for the coin to be called mint state.

Satin Finish – See "Roman Finish."

Select – An adjective which the A.N.A. applies to Mint State or Proof-63 coins.

Semi-Prooflike – A coin which has almost enough mirror-like reflectiveness to be called "prooflike."

Sheldon Scale – A system of grading which was originally introduced by the late Dr. William H. Sheldon, for the purpose of grading large cents. The system was adapted to all coins in the early 1970's. The Sheldon Scale, as used today, incorporates numerical grades 1 through 70 to correspond with various descriptive grades as follows:

Poor-1
Fair-2
Almost Good-3
Good-4, 6
Very Good-8, 10
Fine-12, 15
Very Fine-20, 25, 30, 35
Extremely Fine-40, 45
Almost Uncirculated-50, 55, 58
Mint State- 60, 61, 62, 63, 64, 65, 66, 67, 68, 69, 70

Slab – The plastic holder in which the leading grading services will encapsulate a coin which they have graded.

Sleeper – A coin which is undervalued or underpriced.

Slider – A coin which a less scrupulous individual might sell at a higher grade than it really merits. The term usually refers to a nearly mint state coin which is, or could be offered as a full mint state.

Split Grade – A coin whose obverse grade is different from its reverse grade. Examples: MS-63/65 or Proof 63/60.

Strike – The sharpness of detail which the coin had when it was mint state. A full strike is a coin which exhibits the full detail that would appear on the sharpest known examples of that type.

Technical Grading – A system of grading which only takes into account that which has happened to a coin after the minting process (i.e. the state of preservation). Generally, technical grading is ultra critical of post-minting process imperfections affecting surface preservation and lustre. Technical graders often ignore strike and eye-appeal. Although not always as meaningful in the real marketplace, technical grading tends to be more conservative, as a rule, than market grading.

Toned – An adjective which describes a coin with toning.

Toning – The coloring which has formed on the surface of a coin as a result of the metal's interaction with outside elements. (Synonym: "Patina").

Type – A date or group of dates encompassing all of a particular standard design. (Example: Morgan silver dollars). A type collection is a collection of coins formed by one example (usually one of the most common dates) of each type of coin.

Typical Uncirculated or Proof – A term which the A.N.A. suggests using to describe a Mint State-60 or Proof-60 coin. This is not necessarily the way a coin typically comes. (For example, a typical bag-quality 1881-S dollar is actually closer to Mint State-63).

Wear – Visible erosion of metal, usually beginning from the highest points of a coin. Eventually, details, letters, or entire shapes are obliterated. Wear should not be confused with strike. Sometimes a worn coin can have more detail than a weakly struck mint state coin.

Whizzed – An artificial process whereby the surface of a coin is buffed to give it the appearance of having natural cartwheel lustre.

Wire Rim – An effect whereby a thin, wire-like section of the rim of a coin is raised above the rest of the rim along the outside. This effect is usually caused by very high striking pressure, and tends to occur mostly on proof and high relief strikings.

chapter one

THE GRADING PROCESS

Mint State or Almost Uncirculated?

"See how today's achievement is only tomorrow's confusion."
William Dean Howells

Perhaps the toughest part of the process of grading involves distinguishing between a mint state coin and a top grade Almost Uncirculated (A.U.) coin. Detail is not the only criteria. Sometimes an A.U. coin (or even an Extremely Fine coin) will have better detail than an uncirculated coin. This, of course, is due to the fact that some coins are struck with more detail than others.

Once you know that a coin cannot be graded solely based on detail, you can begin the process of learning how to distinguish wear. Throughout this book, I will use the Morgan Silver Dollar as an example of each grading technique. Toward the end of the book, you will learn how to apply these techniques to other coins.

Below are photographs of the obverse and reverse of a fully struck Morgan dollar. Accented in red are the high points of the design. These are the areas where the wear from circulation is most likely to appear first. Unfortunately, these are also areas which tend to lack detail if the coin is weakly struck or if it was struck from worn dies.

obverse

reverse

The best way to learn to tell if a coin has *wear* is through actual experience. Compare a coin which you know is uncirculated to a slightly circulated (AU) coin with equal detail. Observe the coins carefully, tilting them back and forth to see how the lustre flows, especially over the high points. Look closely at the high points. You will notice a difference in the lustre. On the uncirculated coin, the full lustre will roll over the high points. On the A.U. coin, the lustre will be visibly broken, and this break will be noticeable without magnification. Thus, even to a somewhat inexperienced eye, it will convey the visual impact of slight wear (i.e. displacement of metal).

It is important to note, however, that many mint state coins will have slight "friction" on the high points or in the fields, resulting from coins rubbing against each other in rolls or bags. If the metal itself is not disturbed, and the lustre is intact (with perhaps just the slightest disturbance, usually from very tiny hairlines), the coin is probably still mint state.

This exercise is best performed, at first, using coins which have no toning. Once you have mastered untoned coins, you can try the same thing using toned coins. Just try to look "through" the toning as if it were never there. But I warn you that toned coins are many times trickier than untoned coins.

Now, here's an interesting question: If you remove the toning from a coin, all other things being equal, can that alone change the grade from almost uncirculated to fully mint state, or vice-versa?

The answer, surprisingly, is yes! Even though technically the removal of toning should not (and really does not) affect the presence of wear, it does affect the *visual impact* of wear. Until coins are graded by computer, and possibly even after that, visual impact will be the single most important factor in grading a coin. Sometimes toning will sufficiently hide wear from even the most experienced eye. In some cases, toning will create the illusion of wear to even the most experienced eye. In these rare cases, the illusion becomes the reality, because the market will value those coins based on their visual impact.

The goal, therefore, is not to know exactly how the coin would look if the toning were removed. It is impossible to do that. Even the top experts don't always know what lurks beneath the toning of a coin. The goal is to assess the visual impact of wear on the coin, as accurately as possible.

chapter two

HOW TO GRADE MINT STATE COINS

Like any science, language, sport, or field of study, it is best to break grading down to its basic components, and master them one at a time. I learned how to grade coins much the same way I learned how to speak English; all at once, through experience. In retrospect, however, it seems to me that both topics would be quite a bit easier to learn if one studied them one aspect at a time. This statement is especially true as a person gets older. Hence, most people learn their first language through experience. But if they learn a second language, they learn the rules first, then the vocabulary, then the sentence structures, etc. (Note, however, that by far the most effective way to learn both a second language and coin grading is by learning the rules first, and then combining that knowledge with actual experience. Either subject is nearly impossible to learn entirely from a book.)

Interestingly, it is rare that someone who learns coin grading does so in this way. Most people learn by experience far more than they do by rules, and this is especially true of those who learn to grade mint state coins. I personally have never bothered to learn any "rules" or "components" of grading. Therefore, in the course of writing this book, I have analyzed, for the first time in my life, how I grade coins. What components make up the actual process of grading uncirculated and proof coins? How important is each component in relation to the others?

After much thought, I now believe that the essence of grading a coin (once you have determined that it is definitely uncirculated or proof) can be broken down into four distinct factors:

1. **Surface Preservation** – This includes the presence of bagmarks, hairlines from cleaning or mishandling, and other imperfections of planchet, whether mint caused or man made. An analysis of surface preservation attempts to weigh the visual impact of these imperfections based on their degree of severity and their location on the coin.

2. **Strike** – Refers to the sharpness and completeness of detail, with the normal characteristics of that particular type, date and mint mark (i.e. issue) taken into account.

3. **Lustre** – This encompasses the brilliance, cartwheel, sheen and contrast of the coin, again taking the normal characteristics of the particular issue into account. Minor (non-hairline producing) cleaning, retoning, friction, etc., are evaluated under this category.

4. **Eye-Appeal** – That certain aesthetic appeal that results from the attractiveness of the toning (if any), the balance of the coin, and the effect of the combination of all of the coin's qualities.

I believe that **Surface Preservation** is the single most important factor in grading mint state coins. The other three factors appear to be approximately equal in value, each about half as important as surface preservation. (i.e. 40% + 20% + 20% + 20% = 100%). Actually, this formula is somewhat arbitrary since it is really a function of the standards of the scales we use for each of the factors themselves. I chose this 40/20/20/20 formula mainly for its simplicity. The scales for the individual factors, outlined in the next four chapters, were designed around this formula. With this in mind, I hope to teach you how to properly evaluate each factor, assign a numerical value to that factor, and then turn that information into a valid grade.

You will then learn when to add to this grade such adjectival modifiers as prooflike, full strike, rim nick, weakly struck, cleaned, etc.

In this attempt to analyze each of these four components of grading mint state coins, as I mentioned before, the Morgan silver dollar is used as the example. Once you know how to grade a Morgan dollar, it should be relatively easy to learn to grade other coins. I will try to teach you how to grade the other types mainly by exception. In other words, I will attempt to show how a Saint Gaudens double eagle, or a Barber half dollar is graded *differently* from a Morgan dollar.

chapter three

SURFACE PRESERVATION

As I mentioned in the previous chapter, surface preservation includes the presence of bagmarks, hairlines from cleaning or mishandling, and any other imperfections of planchet, whether mint caused or man made. An analysis of surface preservation attempts to evaluate the **Visual Impact** of these imperfections based on their degree of severity and their location on the coin.

As you look at lots of coins, you will notice that bagmarks tend to be the most common detracting surface problem on most business strikes. Hairlines, on the other hand, are usually the most prevalent detractor of the surfaces of proof coins. This results from the physical differences between business strikes and proof coins, and the different way each type of coin tends to have been handled.

Most business strikes, at one time or another, were shipped in bags. Therefore, nearly all business strikes have some marks caused either by banging against other coins, or by some other form of mishandling after being removed from the bag.

Proof coins were handled much more carefully. Unfortunately, proof surfaces tend to magnify even the lightest mishandling into hairline scratches. Indeed, prooflike uncirculated coins generally have bagmarks **and** hairlines. Therefore, prooflike Morgan dollars tend to be quite a bit rarer in MS-65 grade than frosty Morgan dollars. This is one of the reasons why prooflike gems command higher prices than frosty gem Morgans.

Whenever we analyze the severity of an imperfection of a coin, we try to figure out what visual impact that imperfection will have on the eye of a trained numismatist. Obviously, the more severe the imperfection, which is measured by the amount of displaced metal, the worse the imperfection.

Of course, this statement is only true if we are comparing examples of the same type of imperfection. For example, a hairline is generally far worse than a bagmark of equal metal displacement and location, because hairlines create a lot of visual impact with very little metal displacement.

However, a mint caused planchet defect is usually not as detracting as a bagmark. This is mainly because any mint-caused imperfection is not regarded to be as detrimental as if it were man-made (i.e. post minting process.) Also, very often the lustre will run unbroken through a mint caused planchet defect. This applies to planchet laminations, lint marks, die rust, die wear, or practically any other mint caused defect. (Note: Minor die scratches and clashed dies are not usually considered to be serious defects, and hardly affect the grade, if at all. In many cases, they don't even affect the *value* of the coin). Of course if a mint-caused defect is huge and ugly, it is still far worse than one that's tiny and unobtrusive – just like bagmarks and hairlines. A good rule of thumb is that a mint-caused defect will affect the grade about half as much as a bagmark or hairline of equal visual impact.

Spots, fingerprints and other discoloration, other than on copper coins, usually fall into the eye-appeal category (which will be covered a few chapters later). Most spots are at least partially removable, unless the coin is copper or nickel. However, if the discoloration begins eating into the metal (i.e. corrosion), then this, too, falls under surface preservation. Any corrosion of metal must be rated on visual impact, similar to a hairline or bagmark. NOTE: Major surface impairments such as harsh cleaning, blatantly artificial toning or repairs will prevent most services (including P.C.G.S. and N.G.C.) from issuing a grading opinion at all.

Once you have determined the *severity* of an imperfection, this information must be measured in combination with the *location* of the imperfection. Below is a photograph of a Morgan dollar, color coded as follows:

RED – Worst (Average x 4)
ORANGE – Bad (Average x 2)
YELLOW – Average
GREEN – Better (Average x ½)
BLUE – Best (Average x ¼)

NOTE: These quantifications are *approximate*.

For example, a mark in the red area is about 8 times as serious than if the same mark were in the green area, as illustrated on the photograph below. Notice that the very worst place is the middle of Miss Liberty's cheek. This area is the focal point of the coin, and the one place where experienced numismatists will invariably look first.

obverse

reverse

Also keep in mind that direction of the mark can increase or decrease its effect. For example, a vertical bagmark might be more obvious in Miss Liberty's hair than a horizontal bagmark. A horizontal bagmark would be less noticeable since it would be somewhat hidden and appear to be part of the design at first glance.

The least detrimental area to have an imperfection is on the rim. Rim imperfections tend to be less detracting and less noticeable, because the rim is the least important part of the coin's total design.

Now, the next step is to rate the surface preservation of five mint state and five proof Morgan dollars.

These examples show the worst representations of surface preservation I could find, that could still merit an unqualified MS-60 or Proof-60 grade. Anything worse, and I would have to mention the most prominent defect in my grade description of that coin. (For example, a mint state coin slightly worse than the one pictured here could be described as "MS-60, scratches" or "MS-60, heavy milling marks.")

obverse   Surface Preservation: 1   *reverse*
Business Strike

obverse   Surface Preservation: 1   *reverse*
Proof

obverse   Surface Preservation: 2   *reverse*
Business Strike

obverse Surface Preservation: 2 *reverse*
Proof

obverse Surface Preservation: 3 *reverse*
Business Strike

obverse Surface Preservation: 3 *reverse*
Proof

obverse   *reverse*

Surface Preservation: 4
Business Strike

obverse   *reverse*

Surface Preservation: 4
Proof

obverse   *reverse*

Surface Preservation: 5
Business Strike

obverse   *reverse*

Surface Preservation: 5
Proof

Try to compare any Morgan dollars you wish to grade to these photographs. If you think the surface preservation grades somewhere in between, feel free to use in-between grades like 2-½ or 4-¾, or even 3.79 if you wish to try to be that exact. Remember, at first your grading will involve a lot of guessing. It will take much time and practice before your grading becomes really meaningful. So try to get started practicing as soon as possible.

chapter four

STRIKE

There are several parts of the minting process that could account for the sharpness, or lack thereof, of a coin's strike. The most important aspect is striking pressure. Striking pressure can vary tremendously from coin to coin during the minting process. In fact, some mints (particularly New Orleans, Charlotte and Dahlonega) were usually allocated the poorer condition presses and dies. Therefore these mints tended to produce a worse than average coin in terms of strike. In addition, the sharpness of the die needs to be considered. This may vary due to wear on the die, or on the master die from which the die itself is made. Finally, the consistency and quality of the planchet can affect the quality of strike.

Below is a photograph of a fully struck mint state Morgan dollar:

obverse

reverse

Below are photographs of fully struck examples of some of the various sub-types of Morgan dollar, which show slightly different die characteristics:

obverse

8 Tailfeather
(1878)

reverse

obverse

Flat Breast
(1878)

reverse

obverse

Regular Dies
(1879-1901)

reverse

obverse

New Dies
(1900-1901)

reverse

obverse

Redesign
(1921 only)

reverse

It is important to note that Morgan dollars dated prior to 1879 (including some varieties of 1879-S) and after 1899, simply do not have all the same die details as most Morgan dollars. This variation in no way prevents those coins from being considered fully struck, as long as they possess all the details of their particular sub-type.

Here are photographs of mint state examples of the 1879-1899 sub-type, graded by strike, 1 through 5:

obverse   *reverse*

Strike: 1
(Business Strike)

obverse   *reverse*

Strike: 2
(Business Strike)

obverse

Strike: 3
(Business Strike)

reverse

obverse

Strike: 4
(Business Strike)

reverse

obverse

Strike: 5
(Business Strike)

reverse

35

Note that any coin struck with less detail than the coin in photo #1 must have the weakness of strike somehow noted in its final overall grade description. (For example: MS-63, weakly struck, or MS-60, typical strike for this notoriously weak date.)

Here are photographs of proof examples of the 1879-99 sub-type, graded by strike, 1 through 5:

obverse   reverse

Strike: 1
(Proof)

obverse   reverse

Strike: 2
(Proof)

obverse   Strike: 3   reverse
(Proof)

obverse   Strike: 4   reverse
(Proof)

obverse   Strike: 5   reverse
(Proof)

Again, any coin weaker than photo #1 (regardless of how poorly or well struck that particular issue is normally found) must have the strike mentioned in its overall grade description. Even if this is the case, you should still use the strike grade "1" when calculating the overall grade.

Feel free to use intermediate grades (such as 3-½ or 2.6) when evaluating strike. Also, keep in mind that a coin might have more details than the corresponding photograph in some areas and less details in other areas. Occasionally, a coin may have weakness about the periphery (the outer areas). A good rule of thumb is that it is only about a third (⅓) as detrimental for a coin to lack peripheral detail as it is for the coin to lack the same amount of detail in the central portion.

Here is a brief synopsis of the striking characteristics of each date and mint mark of Morgan dollar. (See footnote #4):

STRIKE

1878	8TF	– Above average to bold.	1885	P	– Above average.
	7/8	– Average.		CC	– Above average to bold.
	7F	– Above average.		O	– Variable, but usually average.
	7F RB	– Sharp and bold.		S	– Average.
	CC	– Sharp and bold.	1886	P	– Usually sharp.
	S	– Sharp and bold.		O	– Weak and soft.
1879	P	– Variable, but generally average.		S	– Usually well struck.
	CC	– Average.	1887	P	– Usually sharp and bold.
	O	– Average to above average.		O	– Variable, often weakly struck.
	S	– Sharp and bold.		S	– Above average.
1880	P	– Average to above average.	1888	P	– Average.
	CC	– Above average to bold.		O	– Average, though many are weak.
	O	– Variable, but generally strong.		S	– Average.
	S	– Sharp and bold.	1889	P	– Average, though some are a bit soft.
1881	P	– Above average.		CC	– Usually sharp and bold.
	CC	– Sharp and bold.		O	– Generally quite weak and soft.
	O	– Average.		S	– Typically sharp and bold.
	S	– Sharp and bold.	1890	P	– Average, though some are soft.
1882	P	Above average.		CC	– Above average to sharp.
	CC	Above average.		O	– Generally weak and soft. P-L's usually above average.
	O	Average.		S	– Most sharp and bold.
	S	Sharp and bold.	1891	P	– Most weak.
1883	P	– Above average.		CC	– Above average.
	CC	– Above average, to bold.		O	– Typically soft and weak.
	O	– Average to a bit soft.		S	– Variable, but most are sharp.
	S	– Sharp and bold.			
1884	P	– Above average to bold.			
	CC	– Above average to bold.			
	O	– Soft to average.			
	S	– Above average.			

1892	P	– Many weak, but variable.
	CC	– Above average.
	O	– Almost always weak and soft.
	S	– Sharp and well struck.
1893	P	– Average to above average.
	CC	– Most are weak, especially P-L's.
	O	– Typically weak.
	S	– Sharp when found.
1894	P	– Usually well struck.
	O	– Generally quite soft.
	S	– Sharp and bold.
1895	P	– Proof only, almost always sharp.
	O	– Weak and soft.
	S	– Above average.
1896	P	– Sharp and bold.
	O	– Weak and soft.
	S	– Usually average.
1897	P	– Generally sharp.
	O	– Average, though some weak.
	S	– Above average.
1898	P	– Sharp and bold.
	O	– Above average.
	S	– Average to above average.

1899	P	– Above average to bold.
	O	– Above average to bold.
	S	– Above average.
1900	P	– Average.
	O	– Average.
	S	– Average.
1901	P	– Generally weak and soft.
	O	– Average.
	S	– Most weak to average.
1902	P	– Variable, though usually well struck.
	O	– Average.
	S	– Weak and soft.
1903	P	– Usually sharp.
	O	– Above average.
	S	– Sharp and bold.
1904	P	– Average, though some a bit soft.
	O	– Average.
	S	– Above average.
1921	P	– Average, though some a bit soft.
	D	– Below average to average.
	S	– Weak and soft.

Note: Any date listed as being normally softly struck, when found exceptionally well struck, may be noted as such in the overall grade description. (For example: MS-60, full strike; or MS-65, sharp strike.)

chapter five

LUSTRE

During the minting process, a planchet becomes a coin once it has been struck between two dies. The striking takes place under extreme pressure. It is this pressure which is responsible for the phenomenon known as mint lustre. Mint lustre, which is a combination of cartwheel, sheen, brilliance and contrast, is defined simply as the way in which the surface of a coin reflects light.

When you grade the lustre of a coin, you basically grade the intensity, beauty and integrity of that coin's ability to reflect light, within the bounds of the lustre characteristics of that issue. For example, a matte proof gold piece has very little, if any, brilliance, cartwheel or contrast. Therefore, the lustre of a matte proof Saint Gaudens $20 must be evaluated purely on the basis of original mint sheen. Such an evaluation will have to be made through experience. Only by looking at several matte proof gold pieces can a neophyte begin to understand the difference between a natural matte sheen, and a cleaned or "dipped out" surface.

For the purpose of this discussion, let us take a common date silver dollar, for example, an 1885-O. First, we examine the highest points, accented in red, as illustrated here:

obverse   *reverse*

Is the lustre as pronounced at the very highest points as it is in the fields? If not, the coin has some "friction," as discussed in the chapter entitled "The Grading Process – Mint State or Almost Uncirculated." There is no visual impact of metal displacement (otherwise the coin would be considered AU), but there is often some disturbance of lustre. The degree of this disturbance will affect your lustre grade.

Next, examine the fields of the coin. Is the lustre absolutely booming, or is it pretty good, just so-so, or plain dull? Don't take the hairlines into account, since you've already accounted for them as part of your surface preservation grade.

However, if the coin has ever been cleaned, retoned, or dipped too often, the lustre will be reduced to some degree. And, of course, some coins are made better than others.

If the coin has virtually no lustre, this must be mentioned in the description (i.e. MS-60, dull; or MS-63, but lacklustre from prolonged immersion in seawater). If any areas on the coin are polished or harshly cleaned, this too must be mentioned in the description.

Now, give the coin a grade of 1 to 5 (fractions are okay) based on its lustre. Make this evaluation with your own experience from looking at other coins of that issue (i.e. type, date and mint mark), while keeping the criteria outlined in this chapter, in mind. The more experience you have had, the more meaningful your grade will be. Even if you have no idea what grade to assign, take a guess. Eventually, your guesses will become closer and closer to 100% accurate.

For your further study, here is a list of the lustre characteristics of the various issues of Morgan dollars (See footnote #4):

LUSTRE

1878 8TF	–	Frosty surfaces, good lustre, occasionally found with one side prooflike.
7/8 TF	–	Frosty surfaces, good lustre, scarce in prooflike.
7 TF	–	Full frosty surfaces, good lustre. Prooflikes are available.
7TF RB	–	Semi-prooflike surfaces, excellent lustre. Seldom found fully prooflike.
S	–	Frosty or semi-prooflike surfaces, excellent lustre. Often found fully prooflike, but heavily bag-marked.
CC	–	Frosty surfaces, good lustre, frequently seen prooflike.

1879 P	–	Frosty surfaces, good lustre, prooflikes not scarce.
O	–	Frosty surfaces, excellent lustre, some prooflikes.
S	–	Semi-prooflike surfaces, excellent lustre. Fairly scarce with deeply reflective fields.
CC	–	Variable. Frosty or semi-prooflike surfaces, poor to good lustre. Heavily marked.
1880 P	–	Frosty surfaces, good lustre. Prooflikes infrequent.
O	–	Frosty surfaces, excellent lustre. Very scarce in prooflike.
S	–	Semi-prooflike surfaces, excellent lustre, readily available in prooflike.
CC	–	Frosty surfaces, good lustre. Scarce in P-L.

1881 P – Frosty surfaces, excellent lustre. Prooflikes are available, but not typically deep.

O – Frosty or semi-prooflike surfaces, good lustre, heavily marked and scarce with deep mirror surfaces.

S – Semi-prooflike surfaces, excellent lustre. Often seen prooflike, but cameo contrast elusive.

CC – Frosty or semi-P-L surfaces, good to excellent lustre. Prooflikes are readily available.

1882 P – Frosty surfaces, good lustre. Fairly scarce in P-L.

O – Frosty or Semi-P-L surfaces. Good lustre. P-L's often heavily marked.

S – Semi-P-L surfaces, excellent lustre. Prooflikes are plentiful, but cameos are tough.

CC – Frosty surfaces, good lustre. Some prooflikes.

1883 P – Frosty surfaces, good lustre. Semi-P-L's around, though full P-L's are scarce.

O – Frosty surfaces, good lustre. Many prooflikes.

S – Semi-prooflike surfaces, excellent lustre.

CC – Frosty surfaces, good lustre. Moderately scarce as P-L.

1884 P – Frosty surfaces, good lustre. Very scarce in true P-L.

O – Frosty surfaces, good lustre. Prooflikes are readily available.

S – Frosty surfaces, good lustre. Prooflikes are rare, as is issue in Mint State.

CC – Frosty surfaces, good lustre. Prooflikes available.

1885 P – Frosty surfaces, good lustre. Prooflikes readily available.

O – Frosty surfaces, good lustre. Semi-P-L's available, but true P-L's scarcer.

S – Frosty surfaces, good lustre. Very scarce in P-L

CC – Frosty surfaces, good lustre. Not difficult in P-L.

1886 P – Frosty surfaces, excellent lustre. P-L's available.

O – Frosty surfaces, poor to good lustre. Very rare with fully P-L surfaces. A few semi-P-L's.

S – Semi-prooflike surfaces, excellent lustre. Full P-L's scarce.

1887 P – Frosty surfaces, excellent lustre. Relatively common in P-L.

O – Frosty surfaces, good lustre. P-L's appear.

S – Frosty or semi-P-L surfaces. Good lustre. P-L's appear, often one-sided.

1888 P – Frosty surfaces, good lustre. Scarce in P-L.

O – Frosty surfaces, good lustre. Scarce in P-L.

S – Semi-P-L surfaces, good lustre. Scarce in true P-L.

1889 P – Frosty surfaces, good lustre. Tougher issue in P-L.

O – Frosty surfaces, good lustre. Very scarce in P-L, especially with mark-free surfaces.

S – Semi-P-L surfaces, excellent lustre. Deep mirror P-L's elusive.

CC – Prooflike surfaces, good lustre. Entire issue quite rare.

1890 P – Frosty surfaces, poor lustre. Very scarce in prooflike, especially with clean surfaces.

O – Frosty surfaces, good lustre. P-L's more common than generally thought.

S – Semi-prooflike surfaces. Excellent lustre. Prooflikes are available.

CC – Frosty surfaces, good lustre. Prooflikes seen with moderate frequency.

1891 P – Frosty surfaces, poor lustre. Seldom seen prooflike.

O – Frosty surfaces, poor lustre. Quite rare in P-L.

S – Semi-prooflike surfaces, excellent lustre. P-L's available.

CC – Frosty surfaces, good lustre. Prooflikes somewhat elusive.

1892 P – Frosty surfaces, poor to good lustre. Full P-L's fairly rare. Semi-P-L's abundant.

O – Frosty surfaces, good lustre. Extremely rare in prooflike.

S – Semi-prooflike surfaces, excellent lustre. P-L's not rare for issue, but whole issue is rare in Mint State.

CC – Frosty surfaces, excellent lustre. Quite scarce in true P-L. Semi-P-L's common.

1893 P – Frosty surfaces, excellent lustre. Extremely rare in P-L, particularly top end condition.

O – Frosty surfaces, good lustre. Very rare with fully P-L surfaces.

S – Semi-prooflike surfaces, excellent lustre. Fully P-L surfaces virtually unknown on Mint State examples.

CC – Frosty surfaces, excellent lustre. P-L's quite scarce, even more so fully struck.

1894 P – Frosty surfaces, poor lustre. Extremely rare in P-L.

O – Frosty surfaces, good lustre. Very rare in P-L, especially nice examples.

S – Frosty or semi-prooflike surfaces, excellent lustre. Not particularly scarce in P-L.

1895 O – Frosty surfaces, good lustre. Quite rare in P-L, but sharply struck when found.

S – Frosty surfaces, excellent lustre. True P-L's elusive, though semi-P-L's are around.

1896 P – Frosty surfaces, good lustre. Relatively common in P-L.

O – Frosty surfaces, poor lustre. Extremely rare in full P-L.

S – Frosty surfaces, good lustre. Very scarce in P-L.

1897 P – Frosty surfaces, good lustre. Moderately scarce in P-L.

O – Frosty surfaces, poor lustre. Extremely rare in P-L.

S – Frosty surfaces, good lustre. Available as P-L.

1898 P – Frosty surfaces, excellent lustre. Moderately scarce in P-L.

O – Frosty surfaces, excellent lustre. Relatively common in P-L.

S – Frosty or semi-P-L surfaces, excellent lustre. Prooflikes available.

1899 P – Frosty surfaces, good lustre. Not difficult to locate with P-L surfaces.

O – Frosty surfaces, excellent lustre. Somewhat scarce as full P-L, though available.

S – Frosty surfaces, good lustre. Occasionally available as P-L.

1900 P – Frosty surfaces, good lustre. Scarce in full P-L.

O – Frosty surfaces, good lustre. Moderately scarce in P-L.

S – Frosty surfaces, good lustre. Prooflikes available from Redfield.

1901 P – Frosty surfaces, poor lustre. Of the highest rarity with P-L surfaces.

O – Frosty surfaces, good lustre. Very scarce in P-L, though well struck and pleasing when found.

S – Frosty surfaces, good lustre. Extremely difficult in prooflike, and when found, is weakly struck.

1902 P – Frosty surfaces, good lustre. Scarce, though available in P-L. Seldom attractive.

O – Frosty surfaces, good lustre. Scarce with fully reflective fields. Available as semi-P-L.

S – Frosty surfaces, good lustre. Very scarce in P-L. Rare in fully struck P-L.

1903 P – Semi-prooflike surfaces, excellent lustre. Full prooflikes are very scarce.

O – Semi-prooflike surfaces, excellent lustre. Full prooflikes are scarce.

S – Frosty surfaces, excellent lustre. Rare as a prooflike.

1904 P – Frosty surfaces, poor lustre. Almost unknown as a full prooflike.

O – Frosty surfaces, good lustre. Common as prooflike.

S – Frosty surfaces, good lustre. Extremely rare as a P-L.

1921 P – Frosty surfaces, good lustre. Moderately scarce as prooflike.

D – Frosty surfaces, good lustre. Very tough to locate in full P-L.

S – Frosty surfaces, poor lustre. Extremely rare in prooflike.

chapter six

EYE-APPEAL

If lustre sounds subjective to you (it really isn't, it just takes a lot of experience to evaluate it) just wait until you learn about eye-appeal. Eye-appeal is, by far, the most subjective aspect of grading.

To give you an idea about the importance of eye-appeal, I will now tell you my favorite rare coin war story. In late 1979, Jerry Cohen (See footnote #5), then a partner in the Abner Kreisberg Corporation, held a coin auction in Los Angeles. It was an especially beautiful sale with many interesting coins. One of the most interesting (and rare) coins in that sale was a 1795 Small Eagle bust dollar, described simply as Uncirculated. It was a **gem** coin with superb surfaces, lustre and strike. Unfortunately, the toning was positively hideous. The coin simply lacked eye-appeal.

The *Coin Dealer Newsletter* listed "bid" that week at $22,500 in MS-65, and most of the top dealers (myself included) were willing to bid somewhere in the $20,000-$25,000 range for the coin. Steve Ivy, my good friend, but also at that time my arch rival (we're now business partners – how the world changes!) bought the coin for $28,000.

I expected him to "dip" the coin to remove the toning, but business was so brisk at that time that he never got around to it. The coin just sat in inventory for the three or four most explosive months in the history of the coin market. Nobody would buy the coin from him because it lacked eye-appeal. "Bid" doubled to $45,000 by February, 1980. After intensive negotiations (lasting less than a minute, I think) I managed to buy that turkey of a coin from Steve for $33,500. In my mind, this was tantamount to a loss for Steve: He had purchased the coin for 25% over bid, and resold it to me at 25% **below** bid. (It is worth noting that grading standards throughout the industry had certainly **not** tightened over that time period.)

I suppose I had some reservations about dipping the coin. Even for an expert, dipping a coin is a risky undertaking. (And I would never recommend that a novice ever dip a coin). What if the toning hid some unpardonable flaw? Or what if the lustre became dull as a result of the dipping? Still; no guts, no glory!

A quick dip in Jewel Luster produced the most stunning, blazing white semi-prooflike gem early U.S. silver coin I had ever seen! Really, nothing had changed except the eye-appeal factor. The coin was transformed from a "technical MS-65" with no eye-appeal, to a wonder coin, a coin that had it all. The coin that Steve couldn't sell now had suitors waiting in line. There were literally half a dozen knowledgeable buyers begging me to give them first shot at the coin. I sold it to a dealer in the Boston area for $137,500. (See footnote #6).

Since eye-appeal can be so important, it is critical that you develop a sense for it – an art critic's eye for the aesthetically pleasing. My best friend, Marc Emory (See footnote #7) probably has the best eye for quality in the coin business today. Marc taught me almost everything I know about eye-appeal. He believes, as I do, that eye appeal can best be divided into three distinct areas: Toning, balance, and that certain inexplicable: aesthetic attractiveness.

First, toning. Here are photographs of five coins, all approximately equal in surface preservation, strike and lustre. They are arranged from worst to best in terms of toning.

obverse   Toning: 1   *reverse*

obverse   Toning: 2   *reverse*

obverse   Toning: 3   *reverse*

obverse   Toning: 4   *reverse*

obverse   Toning: 5   *reverse*

Note that coin #4 is approximately equal in eye-appeal grade to a coin with no toning at all. However, a flawless gem with no toning and uniform texture on both sides can still be given a 5 for eye-appeal.

The best way to grade a coin for eye-appeal is to make your own judgment as to how your coin's toning compares aesthetically to the coins photographed above. Assign a grade, using fractions where appropriate. Give it a 4, if the coin has no toning at all. Then we'll make adjustments for balance and aesthetic attractiveness.

Balance can best be defined as the coin's overall consistency. Does the toning on the reverse match (or at least go nicely with) the toning on the obverse? Is the texture of the surfaces roughly equivalent on both sides, or is the obverse frosty while the reverse is prooflike (for example)? Does the coin have pleasing balance, or is it somehow lopsided?

A good general rule is to add up to a point to the toning score for perfect balance. (Of course, the maximum score is always 5, so don't add anything if you already gave the toning a 5). Or, you can subtract anywhere from 0 to 50% of the toning score for lack of balance, depending on severity. (In no case should the total score be less than 1).

Finally, to the number above, you can make a final adjustment for that indefinable aesthetic attractiveness. Try this little trick I used to use in college to decide which subject to study next. Say I had a choice of studying for a Sociology exam or writing an Economics paper. I would flip a coin: heads for Sociology, tails for Economics. But instead of actually looking to see if the coin would come up heads or tails, I'd try to notice which result I was subconsciously rooting for. If I found myself hoping that tails would come up, I wouldn't even look at the coin. I'd just start writing the Economics paper.

You can do the same thing when you grade eye-appeal. Consider the eye-appeal grade you gave your coin based on toning and balance. Now look at the coin and try to notice exactly how high or low your subconscious thinks that number is. That difference is purely aesthetic, quite subjective, and probably impossible to explain. Yet it's hard to deny its existence, as you will most likely notice it time and time again during the grading process. Just follow your heart, and adjust your final number as you see fit, just so you keep it between 1 and 5.

Eye-appeal is the grading factor about which expert dealers will most often disagree. You know what you like, and I know what I like. Once you have looked at a few thousand coins, your opinion about the eye-appeal grade of a coin will be as valid as mine or anyone else's.

chapter seven

DETERMINING GRADE

Use the following formula, once you have assigned a numerical grade to the surface preservation, strike, lustre and eye-appeal of each side of a coin:

OBVERSE:

Surface Preservation (1-5) _____ x2 = _____

Strike (1-5) = _____

Lustre (1-5) = _____

Eye-appeal (1-5) = _____

OBVERSE TOTAL: _____

REVERSE:

Surface Preservation (1-5) _____ x2 = _____

Strike (1-5) = _____

Lustre (1-5) = _____

Eye-appeal (1-5) = _____

REVERSE TOTAL: _____

Now we relate the following totals to corresponding grades:

5 to 12.99 = MS or Proof-60
13 to 13.99 = MS or Proof-61
14 to 17.49 = MS or Proof-62
17.5 to 18.99 = MS or Proof-63
19 to 20.49 = MS or Proof-64
20.5 to 21.99 = MS or Proof-65
22 to 22.99 = MS or Proof-66
23 to 23.99 = MS or Proof-67
24 to 24.49 = MS or Proof-68
24.5 to 24.99 = MS or Proof-69
25 = MS or Proof-70

For example, a proof coin with an 18 obverse and a 21 reverse could be graded Proof-63/65. However, its **overall** grading would be Proof-63 since a coin's grade is largely determined by its worst side.

Still, usually the obverse of a coin is considered more important than the reverse. The consensus today is that the value of a coin is determined approximately 60/40 obverse to reverse. In other words, the obverse is about 1½ times more important than the reverse. Practically the only exception occurs in the case of certain commemorative coins and patterns. In these cases, it is somewhat ambiguous which side is the obverse. Both sides are of approximately equal importance in these instances.

For this reason, it may sometimes be considered permissible to upgrade the reverse grade a bit if the obverse is toward the upper end of the scale of its grade. For example, a coin with a 20 obverse and an 18.9 reverse might still be graded MS-64. However, a coin with an 18.9 obverse and a 20 reverse (a far more common occurence) must always be graded MS-63.

chapter eight

IS IT PROOF OR BUSINESS STRIKE?

One of the most difficult parts of grading is distinguishing a "first strike" or "proof-like" uncirculated (i.e. business strike) coin from a proof. It is important to remember that "proof" is not a grade; it is a method of manufacture.

Proof coins are graded in a similar manner to business strike coins (i.e. Proof-1 through Proof-70). A coin which exists only as a proof, such as an 1895 Philadelphia mint Morgan dollar (if you believe, as I do, that all business strikes of that issue were melted) that is worn down to Very Good-8 grade, for example, would still merit the grade Proof-8. Of course, some proof coins are impossible to distinguish as proofs once they are worn beyond a certain point. Therefore, circulated proofs may also be graded by their circulated grade level (i.e. VF-20 or AU-50), especially when there is some doubt as to their proof status.

When you attempt to discern between mint state and proof coins, always remember that proofs are specially made coins. They are struck under greater pressure than most business strikes, and usually they are given two or more blows of the die. In addition, they are struck on specially made, polished planchets, using polished dies (in the case of brilliant proofs.)

Therefore, consider the following factors in tandem with each other, for no single factor is enough to make a conclusive decision:

Proof Surface – A brilliant proof should have a mirror surface. In most cases there will be little if any frost (i.e. cartwheel) in the fields. (See footnote #8). There will be full mirror surfaces even in the protected areas of the field, such as between the vertical lines of the shield, in the case of Seated Liberty coinage. Matte and Roman finish proofs will also lack cartwheel, and will have either dull or satiny surfaces.

Of course many business strikes have mirror or prooflike surfaces. Both prooflike business strikes and proofs will usually have some hairlines. However, business strikes are far more likely to have bagmarks as well as hairlines.

Strike – Proofs tend to be somewhat sharper than business strikes. In fact, most proofs are fully struck. There are a number of exceptions however. The most common exceptions in the Morgan dollar series are the proof issues of 1891, 1892 and especially 1893. These dates are often found weakly struck in the centers. (See footnote #9).

Edges – Most proofs will have either square edges, or wire edges in the case of *some* matte and Roman finish proofs. Business strikes usually do not have square or wire edges, as illustrated:

Normal Edge

Square Edge

Wire Edge

Die Variety – Proofs were usually struck from one or two pairs of dies, and these dies were often used solely for proofs. Therefore, any coin struck from proof dies is at least somewhat more likely to be a proof. Die variety, while not conclusive, can be an important factor in determining proof status.

Lint Marks – Proof dies and planchets were usually polished with soft cloths. Occasionally, pieces of lint would adhere to the die or planchet prior to the striking process. Therefore, lint marks are fairly common on proof coins, yet rare on business strikes.

Lint Mark   Scratch

Lint marks are discerniable from scratches because they are more even and uniform in intensity. They tend to be more curved than scratches. Furthermore, unlike scratches, they aren't surrounded by displaced metal.

If you aren't sure if a coin is proof, and it has one or more lint marks, the chances are good that it is a proof.

Learn how to weigh these factors together. Combined with your own experience from looking at coins, you should be able to tell most proofs from most business strikes. Like grading, the attribution, "proof," is at least partially subjective. Experts often disagree about whether a coin was struck as a proof. If you have any doubt, it is best not to buy the coin unless you know your dealer and he is willing to guarantee, in writing, that the coin you are purchasing is indeed a proof. Otherwise, reconsider whether or not you would wish to own a coin which experts may never unanimously attribute as a proof.

chapter nine

PROOFLIKE COINS

The first few hundred coins struck from a new (or newly polished) die will usually exhibit some degree of mirror, or prooflike (abbreviated as "P-L") surface. The degree of prooflike surface may be noted in the grade description. (For example: MS-65, Prooflike . . . MS-65, deep mirror prooflike.)

The degrees of P-L surface may best be enumerated in order of intensity, from least to most, as follows:

1. Satin-like (or satin surfaces)
2. Semi-Prooflike
3. Prooflike
4. Deep mirror prooflike

Deep mirror prooflike (D.M.P.L. or D.P.L., depending on the grading service you use) coins have fields that are nearly devoid of any cartwheel lustre. In addition, the term "cameo" is sometimes used to denote a P-L or proof coin with exceptional contrast. A cameo coin should have mirror fields, and the devices should display mint frost or "cartwheel" with little or no mirror-like reflective qualities.

Use the gauge on the following page to grade the degree of prooflikeness on any Morgan silver dollar. Lay the coin by its edge on the red line, at a 90 degree angle (i.e. perpendicular) to the page. Place the page approximately 18 inches beneath a 60 watt incandescent lamp. Look at the coin from a 45 degree angle, approximately 12 inches away. The highest prooflike grade that a person with normal eyesight can clearly read within the coin's surface is the prooflike grade which applies to that coin.

NOTE: If the coin is toned, it may be somewhat difficult to see through the toning. Therefore, at first, it is best to use the gauge only with untoned coins. Eventually, you will be able to grade the "prooflikeness" of most toned and untoned coins without using the gauge.

DEEPLY P-L

PROOFLIKE

SEMI P-L

SATIN-LIKE

chapter ten

GRADING OTHER SERIES

In this chapter, you will learn how to apply the grading techniques for Morgan silver dollars, to other series of coins. For each major United States type, including commemoratives, this chapter includes a pair of photographs, one of an obverse and one of a reverse, both as well struck as possible. You should consider any coin you encounter that is as well struck as the illustrated example to rate a 5 on the strike scale. For now, you will have to use your best judgment to grade the strike of less well struck examples.

If the type is commonly available as a proof, I have also included photographs of proof obverse and reverse, again as well struck as possible. If you have any doubt as to whether a coin is a business strike or a proof, compare it to the photographs. In most cases, the differences should be clear.

Then you will find another set of obverse and reverse photographs, this time with the high points of the design accented in red. This will help you determine whether the coin is fully mint state or not. Simply reread the chapter entitled "The Grading Process: Mint State or Almost Uncirculated?" if you are still unsure.

There is a final set of obverse and reverse photographs which illustrate the places on the coin where bagmarks, hairlines and other surface impairments are considered most and least detracting. To refresh your memory, you may wish to reread the chapter entitled "Surface Preservation." The color code is as follows:

RED = Worst (Average x4)
ORANGE = Bad (Average x2)
YELLOW = Average
GREEN = Better (Average x½)
BLUE = Best (Average x¼)

NOTE: These quantifications are approximate.

Keep in mind that an important factor to weigh is how well hidden (or obvious) the surface impairment is.

Lustre and eye-appeal are graded the same way for most series as they are for Morgan dollars. Most exceptions apply to all of the issues of each particular metal (copper, copper-nickel, nickel or gold), and will be noted.

Copper Coins

The most important difference when grading copper coins is that spotting is taken into account as part of the "surface preservation" grade as well as the "eye-appeal" grade. When nickel, silver and gold coins acquire toning (and even spotting in some cases), that toning can often be removed with no ill effects. This is rarely the case with copper coins. Hence, most collectors will highly value a copper coin that has its full **original** red copper color.

Illustrated below are three mint state large cents. They are all approximately the same condition, except that one is completely toned (brown), one is partially toned (red and brown), and the third one has no toning at all (brilliant, or full red).

obverse	Brown	*reverse*
obverse	Red & Brown	*reverse*
obverse	Red	*reverse*

Copper coins are graded by color as well as numerically. The colors are Brown (abbreviated BN), Red and Brown (abbreviated RB) and Red (abbreviated RD). The more red a copper coin retains, generally the more valuable it is.

obverse

1800-1808
Draped Bust Half Cent
Business Strike

reverse

obverse

1809-1836
Classic Half Cent
Business Strike

reverse

1809-1836
Classic Half Cent
Proof

obverse　　　　　　*reverse*

1840-1857
Braided Hair Half Cent
Business Strike

obverse　　　　　　*reverse*

1840-1857
Braided Hair Half Cent
Proof

obverse　　　　　　*reverse*

1796-1807
Draped Bust Large Cent
Business Strike

obverse

reverse

1808-1814
Classic Large Cent
Business Strike

obverse

reverse

1816-1839
Coronet Large Cent
Business Strike

obverse

reverse

1839-1857
Braided Hair Large Cent
Business Strike

obverse

reverse

1839-1857
Braided Hair Large Cent
Proof

obverse

reverse

1856-1858
Flying Eagle Cent
Business Strike

obverse

reverse

1856-1858
Flying Eagle Cent
Proof

obverse   *reverse*

1859-1909
Indian Head Cent
Business Strike

obverse   *reverse*

1859-1909
Indian Head Cent
Proof

obverse   *reverse*

1909-Date
Lincoln Cent
Business Strike

obverse

reverse

1909-1917
Lincoln Cent
Matte Proof

obverse

reverse

1864-1873
Two Cent Piece
Business Strike

obverse

reverse

1864-1873
Two Cent Piece
Proof

obverse

reverse

High Points of Design – Copper

Draped Bust
Half Cent

obverse   *reverse*

Classic
Half Cent

obverse   *reverse*

Braided Hair
Half Cent

obverse   *reverse*

obverse   Coronet Large   reverse
Cent

obverse   Indian Head   reverse
Cent

obverse   Lincoln Cent   reverse

Visual Impairment Severity Levels – Copper

obverse　　Classic Half Cent　　*reverse*

obverse　　Flying Eagle Cent　　*reverse*

obverse　　Indian Head Cent　　*reverse*

obverse   Lincoln Cent   *reverse*

Nickel Coins

The only major difference between nickel coins and other coins is that spots are slightly more detracting on nickel than on silver or gold but less detracting than they are on copper coins. This is because spots on nickel are harder to remove than they are from silver or gold.

(NOTE: Copper-nickel coins such a Flying Eagle cents are graded approximately halfway in-between the way copper and nickel coins are each graded.)

1865-1889
Three Cents (Nickel)
Business Strike

obverse　　　　　*reverse*

1865-1889
Three Cents (Nickel)
Proof

obverse　　　　　*reverse*

1866-1883
Shield Nickel
Business Strike

obverse

reverse

1866-1883
Shield Nickel
Proof

obverse

reverse

1883-1912
Liberty Nickel
Business Strike

obverse

reverse

1883-1912
Liberty Nickel
Proof

obverse

reverse

1913 Type One
Buffalo Nickel
Business Strike

obverse

reverse

1913-1938 Type Two
Buffalo Nickel
Business Strike

obverse

reverse

1913-1917
Buffalo Nickel
Matte Proof

obverse   *reverse*

1936-1937
Buffalo Nickel
Brilliant Proof

obverse   *reverse*

1938-Date
Jefferson Nickel
Business Strike

obverse   *reverse*

obverse

1938-Date
Jefferson Nickel
Proof

reverse

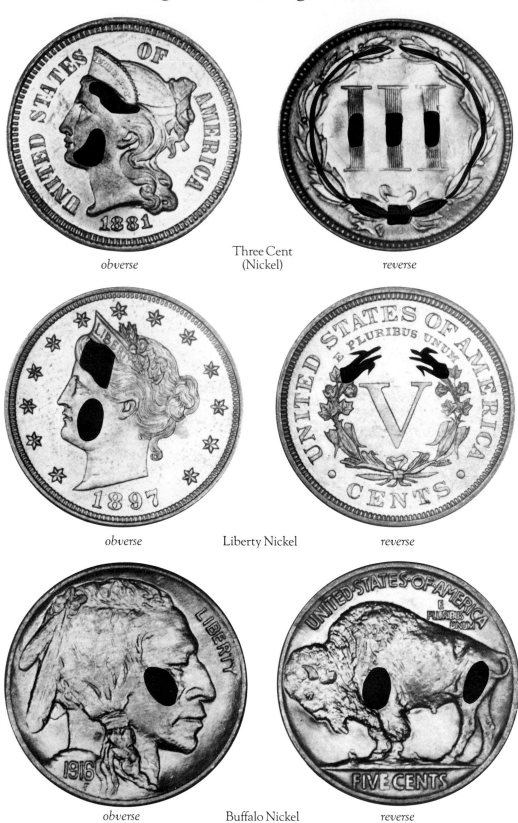

obverse   Three Cent (Nickel)   *reverse*

obverse   Liberty Nickel   *reverse*

obverse   Buffalo Nickel   *reverse*

obverse   Jefferson
                             Nickel   *reverse*

Visual Impairment Severity Levels – Nickel

obverse　　Three Cent
(Nickel)　　*reverse*

obverse　　Shield Nickel　　*reverse*

obverse　　Buffalo Nickel　　*reverse*

Silver Coins

For all practical purposes, you have already learned to grade silver coins. Apply what you have learned about grading Morgan silver dollars to the other silver types illustrated below. The market currently places great emphasis on certain striking characteristics of some series. For example, tremendous premiums are paid for Mercury Dimes with **Full Bands** and Standing Liberty Quarters with **Full Head**. I have included close-up photographs of normal strikes, full bands or full head of the minimum acceptable sharpness and 100% fully struck bands or full head.

Non-Full Bands

Barely-Full Split Bands

100% Fully Struck

Non-Full Head

Barely-Full Head

100% Fully Struck

obverse

1851-1853
Three Cents (Silver)
Type One
Business Strike

reverse

obverse

1854-1858
Three Cents (Silver)
Type Two
Business Strike

reverse

obverse

1854-1858
Three Cents (Silver)
Type Two
Proof

reverse

1859-1873
Three Cents (Silver)
Type Three
Business Strike

obverse

reverse

1859-1873
Three Cents (Silver)
Type Three
Proof

obverse

reverse

1829-1837
Capped Bust Half Dime
Business Strike

obverse

reverse

1837-1838
Liberty Seated Half Dime
No Stars
Business Strike

obverse

reverse

1838-1840
Liberty Seated Half Dime
No Drapery
Business Strike

obverse

reverse

1840-1859
Liberty Seated Half Dime
Stars
Business Strike

obverse

reverse

1840-1859
Liberty Seated Half Dime
Stars
Proof

obverse

reverse

1860-1873
Liberty Seated Half Dime
Legend
Business Strike

obverse

reverse

1860-1873
Liberty Seated Half Dime
Legend
Proof

obverse

reverse

1796-1807
Draped Bust Dime
Business Strike

obverse

reverse

1809-1828
Capped Bust Dime
Large Size
Business Strike

obverse

reverse

1828-1837
Capped Bust Dime
Small Size
Business Strike

obverse

reverse

1838-1840
Liberty Seated Dime
No Drapery
Business Strike

obverse

reverse

1838-1840
Liberty Seated Dime
No Drapery
Proof

obverse

reverse

1840-1859
Liberty Seated Dime
Stars
Business Strike

obverse

reverse

1860-1891
Liberty Seated Dime
Legend
Business Strike

obverse

reverse

1860-1891
Liberty Seated Dime
Legend
Proof

obverse

reverse

1892-1916
Barber Dime
Business Strike

obverse

reverse

1892-1915
Barber Dime
Proof

obverse   *reverse*

1916-1945
Mercury Dime
Business Strike

obverse   *reverse*

1936-1942
Mercury Dime
Proof

obverse   *reverse*

1946-Date
Roosevelt Dime
Business Strike

obverse

reverse

1950-Date
Roosevelt Dime
Proof

obverse

reverse

1875-1876
Twenty Cent Piece
Business Strike

obverse

reverse

obverse

1875-1878
Twenty Cent Piece
Proof

reverse

obverse

1804-1807
Draped Bust Quarter
Business Strike

reverse

obverse

1815-1828
Capped Bust Quarter
Large Size
Business Strike

reverse

1831-1838
Capped Bust Quarter
Small Size
Business Strike

obverse

reverse

1831-1838
Capped Bust Quarter
Small Size
Proof

obverse

reverse

1840-1865
Liberty Seated Quarter
No Motto
Business Strike

obverse

reverse

1840-1865
Liberty Seated Quarter
No Motto
Proof

obverse

reverse

1853
Liberty Seated Quarter
Arrows and Rays
Business Strike

obverse

reverse

1854-1855
Liberty Seated Quarter
Arrows
Business Strike

obverse

reverse

1866-1891
Liberty Seated Quarter
Motto
Business Strike

obverse

reverse

1866-1891
Liberty Seated Quarter
Motto
Proof

obverse

reverse

1892-1916
Barber Quarter
Business Strike

obverse

reverse

1892-1915
Barber Quarter
Proof

obverse *reverse*

1916-1917
Liberty Standing Quarter
Type One
Business Strike

obverse *reverse*

1917-1930
Liberty Standing Quarter
Type Two
Business Strike

obverse *reverse*

1932-Date
Washington Quarter
Business Strike

obverse

reverse

1936-Date
Washington Quarter
Proof

obverse

reverse

1796-1797
Draped Bust Half
Small Eagle
Business Strike

obverse

reverse

1801-1807
Draped Bust Half
Heraldic Eagle
Business Strike

obverse

reverse

1807-1808
Capped Bust Half
Early Style
Business Strike

obverse

reverse

1809-1836
Capped Bust Half
Business Strike

obverse

reverse

1836-1839
Capped Bust Half
Reeded Edge
Business Strike

obverse

reverse

1839-1866
Liberty Seated Half
No Motto
Business Strike

obverse

reverse

1839-1866
Liberty Seated Half
No Motto
Proof

obverse

reverse

95

1853
Liberty Seated Half
Arrows and Rays
Business Strike

obverse

reverse

1866-1891
Liberty Seated Half
Motto
Business Strike

obverse

reverse

1866-1891
Liberty Seated Half
Motto
Proof

obverse

reverse

1892-1915
Barber Half
Business Strike

obverse

reverse

1892-1915
Barber Half
Proof

obverse

reverse

1916-1947
Walking Liberty half
Business Strike

obverse

reverse

97

1936-1942
Walking Liberty Half
Proof

obverse   *reverse*

1948-1963
Franklin Half
Business Strike

obverse   *reverse*

1950-1963
Franklin Half
Proof

obverse   *reverse*

obverse

1794-1795
Flowing Hair Dollar
Business Strike

reverse

obverse

1795-1798
Draped Bust Dollar
Small Eagle
Business Strike

reverse

obverse

1798-1804
Draped Bust Dollar
Heraldic Eagle
Business Strike

reverse

1836-1839
Liberty Seated Dollar
Gobrecht
Proof

obverse

reverse

1840-1865
Liberty Seated Dollar
No Motto
Business Strike

obverse

reverse

1840-1865
Liberty Seated Dollar
No Motto
Proof

obverse

reverse

1866-1873
Liberty Seated Dollar
Motto
Business Strike

obverse   *reverse*

1866-1873
Liberty Seated Dollar
Motto
Proof

obverse   *reverse*

1873-1878
Trade Dollar
Business Strike

obverse   *reverse*

1873-1885
Trade Dollar
Proof

obverse

reverse

1878-1921
Morgan Dollar
Business Strike

obverse

reverse

1878-1921
Morgan Dollar
Proof

obverse

reverse

1921
Peace Dollar
High Relief
Business Strike

obverse

reverse

1922-1935
Peace Dollar
Business Strike

obverse

reverse

1971-1978
Eisenhower Dollar
Proof

obverse

reverse

obverse

Three Cent Silver
Type One

reverse

obverse

Three Cent Silver
Type Three

reverse

obverse

Bust Half
Dime

reverse

obverse   Liberty Seated
Dime   reverse

obverse   Barber Dime   reverse

obverse   Mercury Dime   reverse

High Points of Design – Silver

<table>
<tr><td>obverse</td><td>Capped
Bust Quarter</td><td>reverse</td></tr>
<tr><td>obverse</td><td>Liberty Seated
Quarter</td><td>reverse</td></tr>
<tr><td>obverse</td><td>Barber Quarter</td><td>reverse</td></tr>
</table>

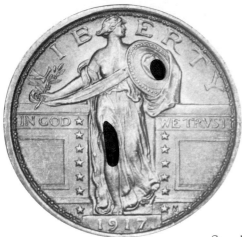

Standing Liberty
Quarter

obverse   *reverse*

Washington
Quarter

obverse   *reverse*

Capped Bust
Half Dollar

obverse   *reverse*

107

Liberty Seated
Half Dollar

obverse *reverse*

Walking Liberty
Half Dollar

obverse *reverse*

Draped Bust
Dollar

obverse *reverse*

obverse   Liberty Seated
Dollar   *reverse*

obverse   Trade Dollar   *reverse*

obverse   Peace Dollar   *reverse*

Three Cent Silver
Type Three

obverse   *reverse*

Capped Bust
Dime

obverse   *reverse*

Liberty Seated
Dime

obverse   *reverse*

obverse · Mercury Dime · reverse

Twenty Cent
Piece

obverse · reverse

obverse · Capped Bust Quarter · reverse

Standing Liberty
Quarter

obverse

reverse

Washington
Quarter

obverse

reverse

obverse

Barber Half

reverse

obverse   Walking Liberty
                      Half   *reverse*

obverse   Franklin Half   *reverse*

obverse   Trade Dollar   *reverse*

obverse   Morgan Dollar   *reverse*

obverse   Peace Dollar   *reverse*

High Points of Design – Silver Commemoratives

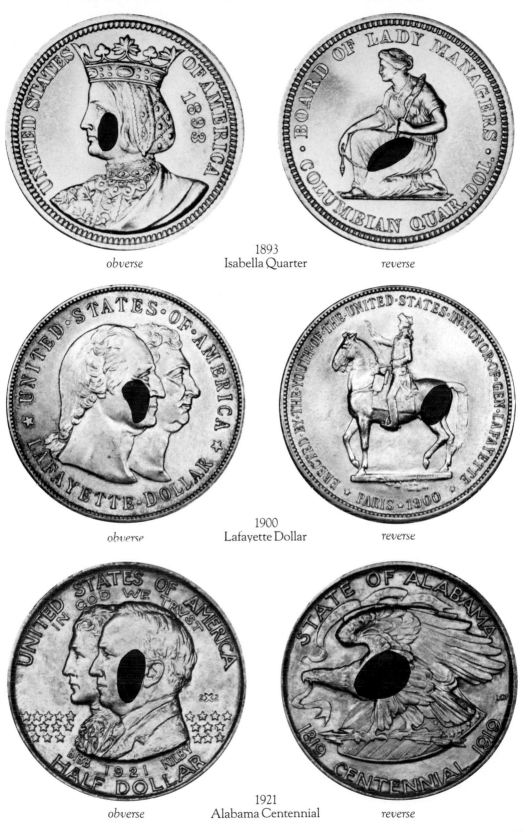

obverse   1893   *reverse*
Isabella Quarter

obverse   1900   *reverse*
Lafayette Dollar

obverse   1921   *reverse*
Alabama Centennial

High Points of Design – Silver Commemoratives

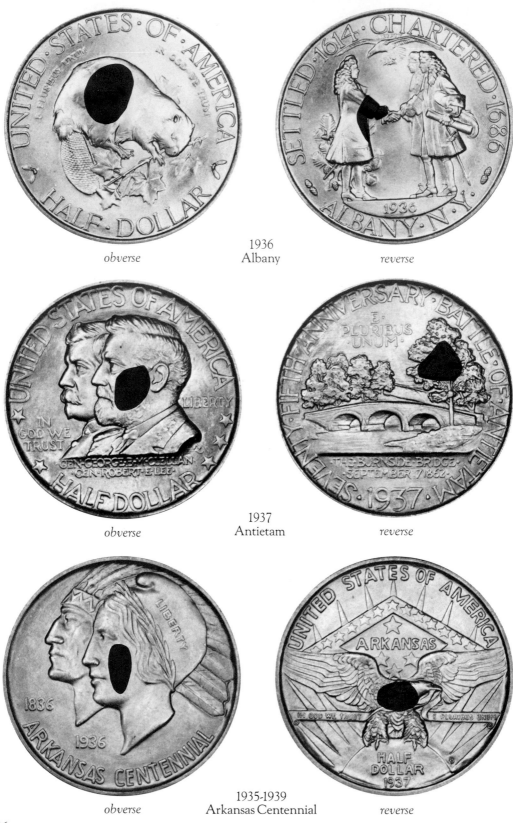

1936
Albany

obverse   *reverse*

1937
Antietam

obverse   *reverse*

1935-1939
Arkansas Centennial

obverse   *reverse*

1936
Bay Bridge

obverse   *reverse*

1934-1938
Boone

obverse   *reverse*

1936
Bridgeport

obverse   *reverse*

High Points of Design – Silver Commemoratives

obverse

1925
California Jubilee

reverse

obverse

1936
Cincinnati

reverse

obverse

1936
Cleveland

reverse

1936
Columbia South Carolina

obverse　　　　　　　　　　*reverse*

1892-1893
Columbian Exposition

obverse　　　　　　　　　　*reverse*

1935
Connecticut

obverse　　　　　　　　　　*reverse*

High points of Design – Silver Commemoratives

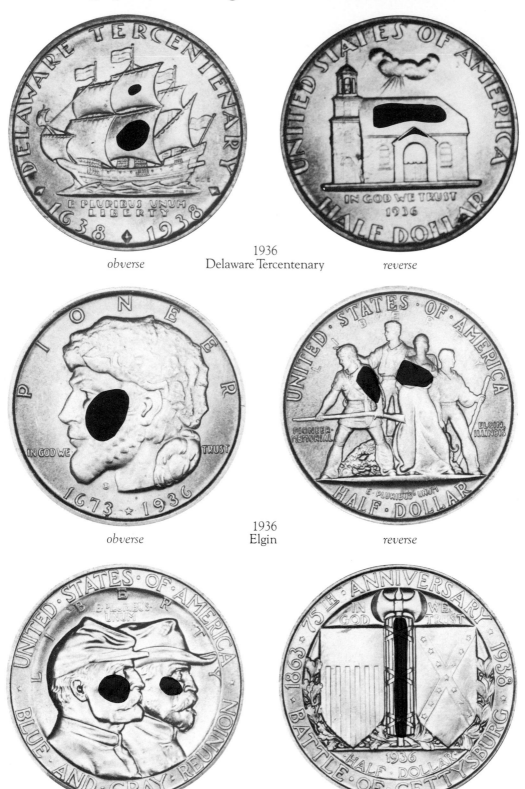

obverse   1936 Delaware Tercentenary   *reverse*

obverse   1936 Elgin   *reverse*

obverse   1936 Gettysburg   *reverse*

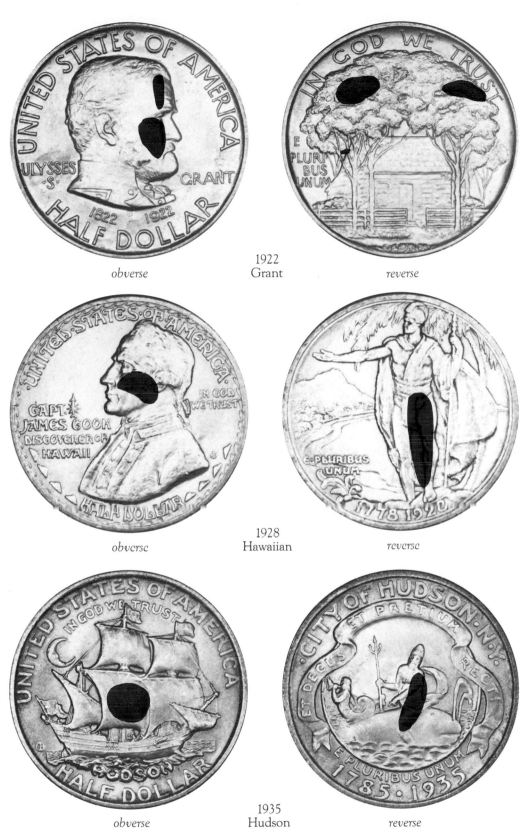

1922
Grant

obverse

reverse

1928
Hawaiian

obverse

reverse

1935
Hudson

obverse

reverse

High Points of Design – Silver Commemoratives

1924
Huguenot-Walloon

obverse *reverse*

1946
Iowa

obverse *reverse*

1925
Lexington-Concord

obverse *reverse*

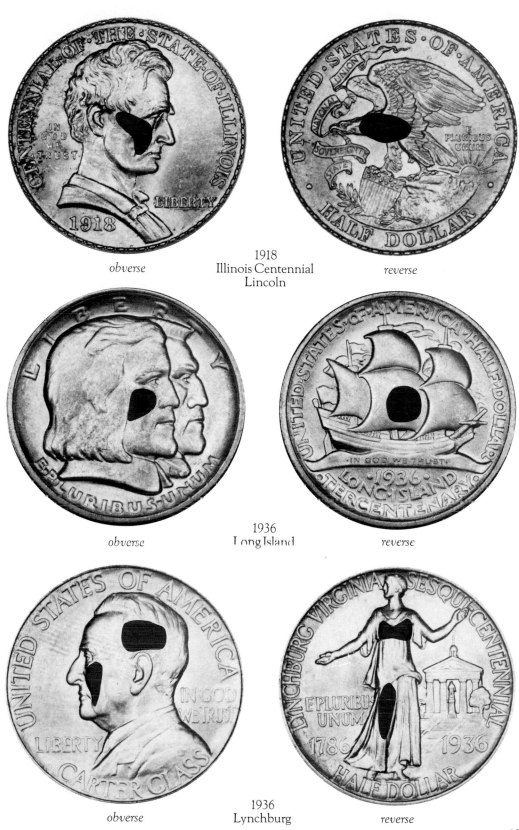

1918
Illinois Centennial
Lincoln

obverse

reverse

1936
Long Island

obverse

reverse

1936
Lynchburg

obverse

reverse

High Points of Design – Silver Commemoratives

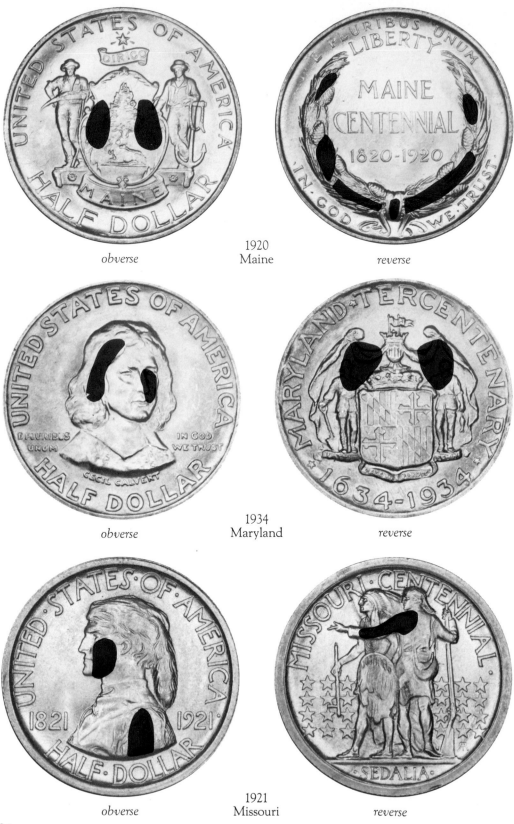

1920
Maine

obverse   *reverse*

1934
Maryland

obverse   *reverse*

1921
Missouri

obverse   *reverse*

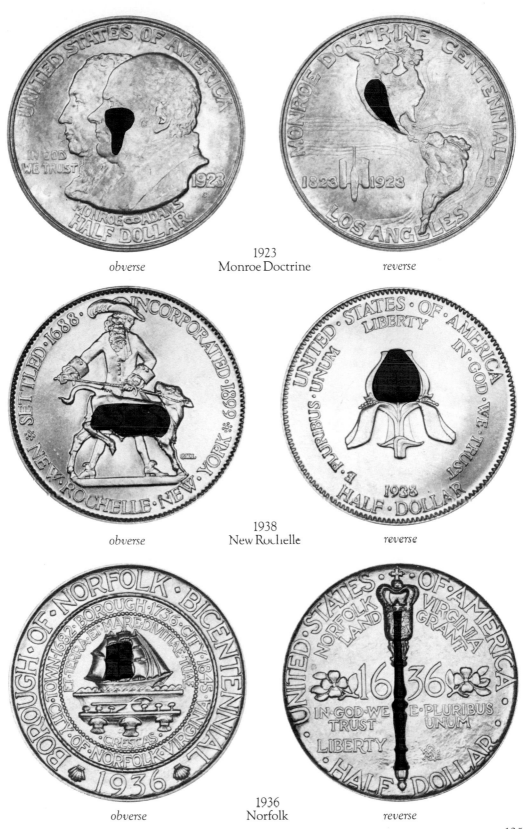

1923
Monroe Doctrine

obverse

reverse

1938
New Rochelle

obverse

reverse

1936
Norfolk

obverse

reverse

1926-1939
Oregon Trail

obverse   reverse

1915
Panama-Pacific

obverse   reverse

1920-1921
Pilgrim

obverse   reverse

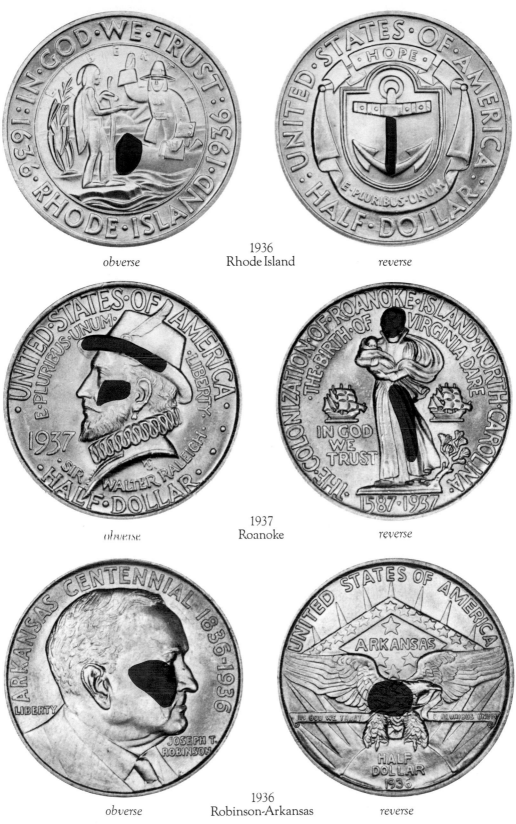

1936
Rhode Island

obverse   *reverse*

1937
Roanoke

obverse   *reverse*

1936
Robinson-Arkansas

obverse   *reverse*

High Points of Design – Silver Commemoratives

1935-1936
San Diego

obverse   reverse

1926
Sesquicentennial

obverse   reverse

1935
Spanish Trail

obverse   reverse

1925
Stone Mountain

obverse   *reverse*

1934-1938
Texas Centennial

obverse   *reverse*

1925
Fort Vancouver

obverse   *reverse*

High Points of Design – Silver Commemoratives

1927
Vermont

obverse   *reverse*

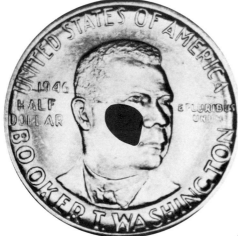

1946-1951
Booker T. Washington

obverse   *reverse*

1951-1954
Washington-Carver

obverse   *reverse*

obverse

1936
Wisconsin

reverse

obverse

1936
York County

reverse

High Points of Design – Gold Commemoratives

obverse

1922
Grant

reverse

High Points of Design – Gold Commemoratives

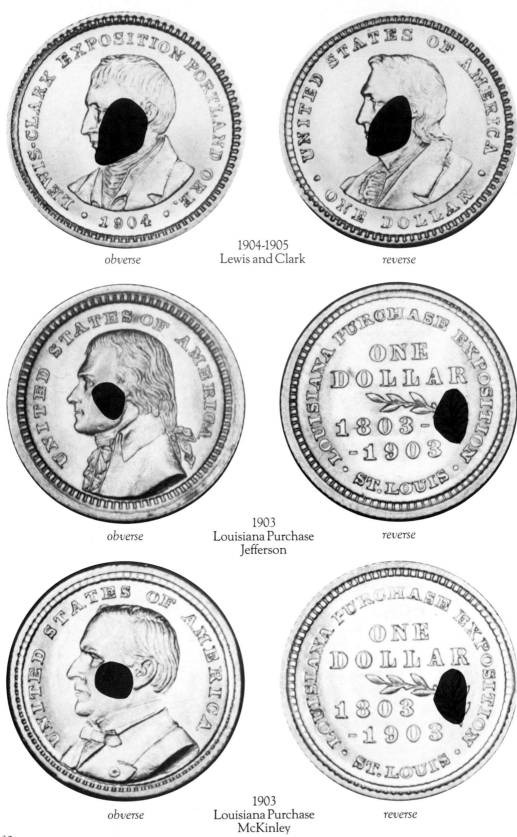

1904-1905
Lewis and Clark

obverse   *reverse*

1903
Louisiana Purchase
Jefferson

obverse   *reverse*

1903
Louisiana Purchase
McKinley

obverse   *reverse*

1916-1917
McKinley Memorial

obverse *reverse*

1915
Panama-Pacific Exposition

obverse *reverse*

1915
Panama-Pacific
Quarter Eagle

obverse *reverse*

High Points of Design – Gold Commemoratives

obverse

1926
Sesquicentennial
Quarter Eagle

reverse

Gold Coins

Gold seldom holds a fingerprint. Spotting on gold coins is often removable and usually detracts little from the grade even when it's not removable.

Sometimes gold coins acquire a beautiful orange-red hue. This coloring is considered by most numismatists to be the most desirable type of toning on gold coins. Attractive, well balanced orange-red toning on gold coins generally merits a 5 on the eye-appeal scale.

1849-1854
One Dollar Gold
Type One
Business Strike

obverse   *reverse*

1854-1856
One Dollar Gold
Type Two
Business Strike

obverse   *reverse*

1856-1889
One Dollar Gold
Type Three
Business Strike

obverse

reverse

1856-1889
One Dollar Gold
Type Three
Proof

obverse

reverse

1834-1839
Classic Quarter Eagle
Business Strike

obverse

reverse

136

1840-1907
Liberty Quarter Eagle
Business Strike

obverse

reverse

1840-1907
Liberty Quarter Eagle
Proof

obverse

reverse

1908-1929
Indian Quarter Eagle
Business Strike

obverse

reverse

1908-1915
Indian Quarter Eagle
Proof

obverse

reverse

1854-1889
Three Dollar Gold
Business Strike

obverse

reverse

1854-1889
Three Dollar Gold
Proof

obverse

reverse

1879-1880
Four Dollar Gold
Stella
Proof

obverse

reverse

1795-1807
Capped Bust Right
Half Eagle
Business Strike

obverse

reverse

1807-1812
Capped Draped Bust
Half Eagle
Business Strike

obverse

reverse

1813-1829
Capped Head Left
Half Eagle
Business Strike

obverse

reverse

1834-1838
Classic Half Eagle
Business Strike

obverse

reverse

1839-1866
Liberty Half Eagle
No Motto
Business Strike

obverse

reverse

1866-1908
Liberty Half Eagle
Motto
Business Strike

obverse   *reverse*

1866-1908
Liberty Half Eagle
Motto
Proof

obverse   *reverse*

1908-1929
Indian Half Eagle
Business Strike

obverse   *reverse*

obverse

1908-1915
Indian Half Eagle
Proof

reverse

obverse

1797-1804
Capped Bust Eagle
Business Strike

reverse

1838-1907
Liberty Eagle
Business Strike

obverse

reverse

1838-1907
Liberty Eagle
Proof

obverse

reverse

1907
Indian Eagle
Wire Edge
Business Strike

obverse

reverse

obverse

1907-1908
Indian Eagle
No Motto
Business Strike

reverse

obverse

1908-1933
Indian Eagle
Motto
Business Strike

reverse

obverse

1908-1915
Indian Eagle
Motto
Proof

reverse

obverse

1849-1866
Liberty Double Eagle
No Motto
Business Strike

reverse

obverse

1866-1876
Liberty Double Eagle
Twenty D.
Business Strike

reverse

obverse

1877-1907
Liberty Double Eagle
Business Strike

reverse

obverse

1877-1907
Liberty Double Eagle
Proof

reverse

obverse

1907
St. Gaudens Double Eagle
High Relief
Business Strike

reverse

obverse

1907-1908
St. Gaudens Double Eagle
No Motto
Business Strike

reverse

1908-1933
St. Gaudens Double Eagle
With Motto
Business Strike

obverse

reverse

1908-1915
St. Gaudens Double Eagle
With Motto
Proof

obverse

reverse

obverse

One Dollar Gold
Type One

reverse

obverse

One Dollar Gold
Type Two

reverse

obverse

One Dollar Gold
Type Three

reverse

obverse

Classic Head
Quarter Eagle

reverse

obverse

Liberty Quarter
Eagle

reverse

obverse

Indian Head
Quarter Eagle

reverse

149

obverse Three Dollar Gold *reverse*

obverse Liberty Eagle *reverse*

obverse Indian Eagle *reverse*

obverse

Liberty Double
Eagle

reverse

obverse

Saint-Gaudens
Double Eagle
(High Relief)

reverse

Visual Impairment Severity Levels – Gold

One Dollar Gold
Type One

obverse　　　　　　　　*reverse*

Indian Quarter
Eagle

obverse　　　　　　　　*reverse*

Liberty Half
Eagle

obverse　　　　　　　　*reverse*

Indian Half
Eagle

obverse   *reverse*

Liberty
Double Eagle

obverse   *reverse*

Saint-Gaudens
Double Eagle

obverse   *reverse*

chapter eleven

WHY WON'T THEY GRADE MY COIN?

You've waited almost two months to get your coins back from the grading service. You open the package, hoping that your treasures have received the high numerical grades they (and you) so richly deserve. But alas, some of your coins aren't in slabs – they're not even graded at all. These coins have been returned to you in a flip similar to the one you used to submit the coin. Your check has been cashed and there is no refund enclosed. "They didn't grade my coins AND they kept my money." you think to yourself, "A grave injustice has been done!"

In reality, it's not an injustice. More work has probably gone into NOT grading your coins than would have gone into grading them. For a variety of good reasons, PCGS, NGC, ANACS and Hallmark will not encapsulate certain coins. (ANACS will, however issue certificates for these coins. NCI will certify AND Encapsulate these coins with the appropriate adjectival modifiers).

This doesn't mean that these coins are worthless. Far from it. It just means that the grading service has decided in the interest of preservation of the coin, protection of value, or sight-unseen trading that the coin should not be slabbed.

There are currently ten different categories of "nograde" classifications currently in use by PCGS. If a coin falls into one or more categories, it will be returned unslabbed. These categories are:

1. **Questionable Toning/Color –** This was formerly referred to as ARTIFICIAL toning or color, but since there is so much controversy and subjectivity about this, the designation was changed. In fact, there are some toned coins that are virtually impossible to determine whether they are toned naturally or artificially.

   Furthermore, there is considerable disagreement over what is natural and what is artificial. Everyone agrees that a coin that is intentionally dipped in Clorox until it turns purple is artificially toned. And nearly all experts agree that a coin that was dipped 10 years ago, and left to tone naturally in a coin album or envelope is a naturally toned coin. But what about a coin that has been left out in the sun in an envelope for a few weeks? How about in an oven for four minutes?! Now you see the problem.

   The graders who work at the grading services see every type of chemically related numismatic horror. They constantly see coins that have been toned with cigar smoke, sulfur, shoe polish and just about everything else ever thought up by a coin dealer's devious mind. Dealers are constantly trying to tone coins in such a way as to cover up defects or otherwise cause their coins to receive higher grades. The attempts people use to trick the graders are diverse, numerous and relentless. Graders are only human, and humans make mistakes. All the major grading services have graded some artificially toned coins, and have had to repurchase those coins. Naturally the graders responsible have been called to the carpet for their mistakes so it is understandable that some graders have gotten "gun-shy" of all toned coins. A few have become downright paranoid, and question the toning on coins that are absolutely original.

Most of the time, the grading services can tell if the toning on a coin is natural or artificial. Still, it can be pretty maddening to buy a 1915 proof set from a family that has held the set since Great-Granddad purchased it in 1915, and have some of the coins come back "Questionable toning." But it happens. So you grit your teeth, spend another submission fee and send the coin back. Or send it to another grading service. It's just a cost of playing the game.

2. **Cleaning** – As recently as the early 1980's, a fully struck choice coin that had been lightly cleaned might sell for 20 to 30% less than the same coin if it were completely original. Today, since that coin will most likely never make it into a slab, it probably trades for 20 to 30% OF (i.e. 70 to 80% off) the price of an original coin in the same grade.

   Severity of cleaning is very important, as is eye-appeal. A coin that was lightly wiped and has since attractively and naturally toned back will almost always be graded. A coin that has been polished or harshly cleaned stands little or no chance of being slabbed.

3. **Planchet Flaw** – Raised metal, missing metal, peeling metal and annealed planchets are just a few of the mint made flaws which, if large enough, will disqualify a coin from encapsulation.

   Grease in the dies, clashed dies, die cracks and die scratches are another story. The grading services will almost always grade coins with these problems, even if they are rather severe. However, if these problems detract from the coin's appearance, the services might lower the final grade by a point or two.

4. **Altered Surfaces** – The Coin Doctor strikes again! That mischevious devil tries to cover a coin's defect to trick the graders into a higher grade. A coin with altered surfaces has generally had a foreign matter applied to it. Currently auto body putty seems to be the substance of choice. Some coin doctors will frost (almost literally paint) the cheek of a Morgan dollar in order to hide facial marks or make them appear less severe. It takes a lot of practice to tell when this has been done, but a good tip-off is when the bagmarks on the cheek appear to be nearly as frosty as the cheek itself.

5. **Scratch** – Location is extremely important here. A half inch scratch on the reverse of a Morgan dollar between the denticles and the lettering will usually cause the coin to be downgraded a point or two. That same scratch across the cheek of Ms. Liberty will probably render the coin ungradable. If you were bidding on MS-65 Morgan dollars sight unseen, would you want to receive one where the first thing you notice is a half inch scratch in the center of the obverse? I didn't think so.

6. **Rim Nick** – A minor rim nick might cause a coin to be downgraded a point or two. A severe rim nick will cause a coin not to be graded. Obviously, the smaller the coin is, the less severe a rim nick is allowed to be in order for the coin to remain gradable.

7. **Environmental Damage** – This is a catchall phrase for any defect which isn't mint caused, and isn't covered in the other categories. Some examples include corrosion, porosity, and PVC that has eaten into the coin's metal. Many gold coins have been recovered from shipwrecks, and some of these coins have been damaged by currents in the salt water which can create a sandblast effect.

8. **Damage** – Coins exhibiting unusual damage such as re-engraving of detail, initials scratched onto the coin, solder on the rim, or heavy and/or numerous cuts, digs or scratches.

9. **Questionable Authority/Not Genuine** – A coin deemed to be a

counterfeit or reproduction. Most of these aren't even legal to own.

10. **PVC** – A coin designated as having PVC (polyvinylchloride) if caught early enough can be easily remedied. PVC leaves a slimy or oily greenish film which can usually be removed by dipping the coin either in acetone or Trichlorotriflouroethane Neutral Coin Solvent (available from E & T Kointainer Co., Box 103, Sidney, Ohio, 45365).

   Many coins stored in soft vinyl flips, that are not inert, experience a chemical reaction and the ensuing PVC problem. If a coin you submit is returned due to PVC, you probably have nothing to worry about. It takes many years (often decades) for PVC to permanently damage most coins. The major grading services don't encapsulate coins with even minor traces of PVC. This is simply because they don't want this damage to occur *after* the coins are in their holders (for obvious reasons).

PCGS and most other serivces allow you to resubmit any coin rejected due to PVC, for only $10.00. Just remove the PVC, and resubmit the coin along with the PVC flip.

11. **Minimum Grade** – This one is obvious. If you submit a coin and specify that it is not to be encapuslated unless it received your designated minimum grade, it won't be; but you still must pay the submission fee, since the coin went through the grading process.

NGC utilizes all of the above-mentioned "no grade" categories. In addition, NGC will not grade any coin dated 1965 and later or any Territorial coinage.

Hallmark utilizes all of the above-mentioned "no grade" categories.

ANACS utilizes all of the above-mentioned "no grade" categories on coins submitted for encapsulation. ANACS, like NCI, will grade impaired coins when a photo certificate is requested and will note the appropriate problem on the certificate.

ANACS will not accept for encapsulation Modern Proof coinage dated 1956 and later with two exceptions: error coins, and those proofs from 1956 – 1965 which merit the CAMEO superlative. Presently, ANACS does not have apertures to fit the Panama-Pacific $50 commemorative. These may be submitted only for the photo certificate option.

NCI will grade many coins the other services will not, but will usually state on the grading certificate and/or slab the specific problem the coin exhibits. NCI believes that the coin still has a grade, but the fact that the coin has been highly cleaned, restored, has a planchet flaw, bad scratch, rim nick, or solder, to name just a few, must also be noted next to the grade on the certificate. In some instances, the coin is downgraded because of the problem.

NCI, NGC, ANACS, Hallmark, and PCGS will not, under any circumstances, grade coins that are questionable as to authenticity.

chapter twelve

HIGH END VS. LOW END

The Bust-Out Game

Only a very tiny percentage of all coins in PCGS, NGC or other similar holders are likely to be graded higher by those services if broken out and resubmitted. A larger (though still relatively small) percentage, if broken out and resubmitted, are likely to be graded lower. This is because most of the coins on the market which the experts consider undergraded have already been resubmitted. Obviously, the more valuable a coin is, the more likely it is to have been resubmitted the optimal number of times to receive its ultimate grade.

To illustrate, let's imagine a coin which three graders out of ten would consider MS-65. The other seven would grade it MS-64. Based on probability statistics there is approximately a one in five chance that a random selection of 3 graders from this mix will result in at least 2 of the 3 graders grading the coin MS-65 thus insuring an MS-65 rating by PCGS or NGC. If the coin is worth $50 in MS-64 and $150 in MS-65, most dealers would just sell it in the MS-64 holder – possibly as a PQ. But, if the coin is worth $300 in MS-64 and $1,000 in MS-65, chances are the dealer will resubmit it until the grading service finally grades it MS-65.

Needless to say, given the cost in time and fees of resubmissions, a dealer's ability to predict how other experts would grade a particular coin is very important to the bust-out game. Since the vast majority of coins would grade the same and some coins would grade lower only a few dealers can consistently make this a profitable venture. As an example, consider for a moment the above example. If one more person out of the 10 had graded the coin MS-64, this would have changed the odds to about one in eighteen, rendering most bust-out scenarios unprofitable.

Note: The consumer is probably not harmed by this, because the market takes this bust-out activity into account. Obviously, if a coin could never be broken out of a holder once sealed, MS-65's would be considerably rarer than they are now. The prices bid on the ANE system would be much higher as a result. Therefore, if a buyer purchases a coin based on the prices reported today on ANE (or any other sight-unseen bidding system), suffice it to say that he (or she) is only paying for a "low-end" coin that has most likely achieved its ultimate grade.

chapter thirteen

COMPUTER GRADING

And what does the future have in store for the grading of coins? Will coins ever be processed through a grading center on a long conveyer belt, subjected to laser inspection, fingerprinted by image analysis, and sealed in a tamper-proof case, all without human intervention?

What will happen to my "wonder toned" coin? Can a computer objectively state that one coin is superior to another based on color? Who said one color is more eye appealing than another? Is this just another way to de-humanize the collector?

These are all common questions asked on the bourse floor whenever the subject of computer grading is discussed. All are legitimate questions that need answers. But before we address these questions, let's first look at what's currently going on in the marketplace.

On May 16, 1990 PCGS announced a major breakthrough in a computerized system that grades coins. The system, PCGS Expert, utilizes robotics, image enhancement, image processing and an online image database for its integrated computer system. The system will perform four primary functions:

1. automated computer grading of coins
2. computer aided grading
3. image archiving
4. digital fingerprinting

1. The most important aspect of the system is the automated computer grading. According to PCGS, the Expert goes through a nine step process before a final grade is assigned to a coin. These steps are:

   1. Multiple images of the coin under various lighting conditions are captured in digital form using a high resolution camera.

   2. All or various portions of the captured images are computer enhanced to bring out important features of the coin.

   3. The key regions of the coin are examined in great detail to identify, classify, measure, and score all flaws.

   4. Secondary regions of the coin are examined to identify flaws that exist in busy background regions such as hair, letters, and rim. These flaws are then classified, measured and scored.

   5. A light flow and reflectance analysis is used to precisely measure the mirror as well as the inherent lustre of the coin.

   6. Key areas of the coin are examined to measure the strength of the strike including the hair.

   7. Thousands of parameters are generated from the various analyses and these are then synthesized into the key components of the coin including obverse and reverse marks, strike, lustre, eye appeal, mirror, toning, and exceptional conditions.

   8. The results are combined using a large set of "expert rules" to establish the final grade.

The process by which PCGS grades has been well thought out, but there will be a need to compare the finished product with the one that is already there. There will be some worry that there may be one trading level for computer graded coins and another for coins already graded.

Initially, PCGS grades Morgan Dollars by computer and will first concentrate on developing computer grading for coins with high submission volumes such as $20 Saint-Gaudens, Walking Liberty Halves, and Proof Franklins.

Here are the other aspects of the computer grading which might become just as important:

2. Computer aided grading will be used in special circumstances to aid the human graders in making a final determination of the grade of the coin.

3. Image archiving will store one or more images of the coin for future reference. This storage method will aid the development of computer grading of coins with smaller populations.

4. Digital fingerprinting will provide additional support in the determination of the authenticity of a coin and will aid in the determining if a coin has been tampered with. It will also be a useful tool for positively identifying coins for the title disputes and other purposes.

An important aspect of their announcement was that PCGS will, for now, utilize a human verifier on all coins graded by the Expert system.

Several other companies are also involved in the development of computer grading. They include such diverse groups as Amos Press (*Coin World*), and CompuGrade, a New Orleans-based numismatic research and development entity. All of the current grading services besides PCGS have expressed interest in computer-grading, but so far no other system has been developed.

Now let's answer some of the questions that we originally discussed.

On the positive side, computer grading systems can be highly consistent, often achieving rates as high as 90%. This is more accurate than any **single** human grader. By using digital fingerprinting, the service can keep records on all of the coins that they have graded. A "grading set" containing several hundred examples is far superior to that of one that contains one or two examples.

The computer grading systems can also be quite cost effective. The human resources that are currently used to grade coins are expensive, and are subject to time limitations in the amount of work they can do in a day. A technician can operate a computer for long periods of time, enabling turn-around time and cost to come down. (Whether or not the services pass along these savings to the consumer depends on the extent of competition in the marketplace).

Now for the negative: Do we really need to have such sophistication for what is essentially a hobby? A lot of people scoffed at David Hall when he first introduced PCGS. But look how far we have come in the last four years. Grading has finally become better defined, and people have taken a stand behind their grades. Computer grading is a natural evolution in the grading process. Its acceptance in the marketplace will be determined by the consumer. If it is able to grade at high degrees of consistency, and at the same time reduce costs to the consumer, then it will be a welcomed addition. If not, it won't be accepted at all.

Can a coin's eye appeal be judged by a computer? At this time the answer is no. This is truly a subjective analysis, that may be resolved with time.

Should we accept computer grading as an integral part of numismatics? The answer is a qualified yes. The fact is that we couldn't stop progress even if we wanted to. So, use the computer wisely, but realize that right now it works best along side human beings.

Footnotes

1. At that time, Jim Ruddy was one of the most prominent figures in numismatics. He was 50% owner of the prestigious numismatic firm of Bowers & Ruddy Galleries, Los Angeles, California. His partner, Q. David Bowers, is currently a principal in Bowers & Merena, Wolfeboro, N.H., the successor firm to Bowers & Ruddy. Dave is certainly the most prolific writer in numismatics, (and an extremely entertaining one!) with literally hundreds of books and articles to his credit, including the introduction to the official A.N.A. Grading Guide. Jim Ruddy is now retired from the coin business.

2. Under the numismatic direction of David Akers, Paramount International Coin Company was perhaps **the** most influential force in numismatics in the early 1970's. Aside from being one of the most active dealers, Paramount provided Coin World with its popular "Trends" pricing guide until July, 1982. Coin World "Trends" was followed even more closely by dealers during the early 1970's than was the Coin Dealer Newsletter. It is my belief that Dave Akers, more than any other individual, was responsible for the introduction of the Sheldon Scale to the entire U.S. numismatic marketplace.

3. Out of concern that readers were becoming confused by terminology being used to describe coins, *Coin World* set forth a policy for advertising Uncirculated coins beginning with the July 3, 1985 issue. That policy states:

    "Because of the number of generally accepted grading standards in use today, *Coin World* has adopted minimum standards for grading terms used in *Coin World* advertisements for Uncirculated coins in order that buyer and seller can better communicate.

    *Uncirculated, Brilliant Uncirculated or Select Uncirculated must be a minimum of Mint State 60.

    *Choice Uncirculated or Choice Brilliant Uncirculated must be a minimum of Mint State 63.

    *Gem Uncirculated or Gem Brilliant Uncirculated must be a minimum of Mint State 65.

    *Superb Gem Brilliant Uncirculated or Superb Brilliant Uncirculated must be a minimum of Mint State 67.

    *Split grades such as MS-63/65 or MS-60/63 must fall back into the lowest adjective level. MS-63/65 may be described as Choice Brilliant Uncirculated or Choice Uncirculated. The split grade MS-60/65 or MS-60/63 may be explained as Uncirculated, Brilliant Uncirculated or Select Uncirculated."

    The operative word is *minimum* in *Coin World's* policy. Thus, choice could apply to either MS-63 or MS-65.

4. Striking and lustre characteristics of each date and mint mark of Morgan silver dollar are paraphrased from the following two publications: *The Bruce Amspacher Investment Report*, P.O. Box 9527, Newport Beach, California 92658, Subscription: $79 per year (10 issues). *What Every Silver Dollar Buyer Should Know*, by Steve Ivy & Ron Howard, available for $19.95 from: Ivy Press, Heritage Plaza, Highland Park Village, Dallas, Texas 75205.

5. My friend Jerry Cohen, and his then-partner, Abner Kreisberg, have handled some of the finest collections ever sold. These include the fabulous "Beck" estate, one of the finest U.S. gold holdings ever to be offered at public auction. The sale discussed in this book was the "Herbert Bergen" Sale, October 4-6, 1979. Jerry and Abner

have since ended their partnership and as of this writing, are both still active in numismatics, in Beverly Hills, California.

6. As an interesting aside, the coin was graded MS-65 by PCGS in 1990, and sold at auction for $418,000. I won't tell you about any of the "rips" Steve Ivy has purchased from me. He'll probably mention some of them in *his* next book. Suffice it to say, that was the last time I ever made a six figure profit on a single coin until 1989. Lest you think the coin business is too easy, I managed to eclipse that record later in 1980, by *losing* $160,000 on a coin! It was a unique plain edge ultra-high relief $20 Saint Gaudens, purchased from Stack's as part of a group of coins in April, 1980, for $1 million. I figured the coin at $375,000, and was offered close to that amount right after the purchase. The market promptly collapsed later that month, and in August, 1980, I accepted an offer of $215,000 from John Dannreuther of Memphis, Tennessee. Today, the coin would probably bring seven figures. (John is a New England Rare Coin Galleries alumnus and is presently one of the leading coin wholesalers in the U.S. as well as a founder of P.C.G.S.)

7. Marc Emory is the most brilliant person I know (taking all of the many different possible types of intelligence into account). Marc has an incredible talent for discerning the slightest nuances of sight or sound. He is the most consistent coin grader I've ever seen. He also speaks eight or nine different languages, all with such fluency and a flawless accent so that natives usually believe he's one of them. If that isn't enough, he's a superb musician. He has made several record albums of his music and occasionally, for fun, performs folk guitar concerts in Germany to sellout crowds. Marc presently lives with his wife, Elisabeth, and two beautiful daughters, Jennifer and Rebecca, near Dusseldorf, West Germany. There he runs the European division of Heritage Rare Coin Galleries. I'm proud to say we've worked together in the coin business continuously since 1975.

8. Some issues are exceptions to this rule. A notable example would be the proof coins of 1860 in *all* denominations. For some reason, most 1860 proof coins display a lot of cartwheel, although their surfaces are still mirror-like.

9. Proof coins of just about all denominations (the main exceptions being the copper issues and three cent silvers) from the years 1868 through 1872 are commonly seen weakly struck in the centers as well.

Conclusion

I hope you have enjoyed reading this book as much as I enjoyed writing it. Tremendous time and effort have gone into fashioning and writing *How to Grade U.S. Coins*. Still, I know that it is still far from perfect. Grading uncirculated and proof coins is a complicated subject, and many details which seem insignificant can make a substantial impact on the final grade.

I'd like to try to improve this book in the future. Therefore, I would be delighted to hear from any readers who feel they can offer suggestions to improve even the most minute details within this book. Please address all comments and suggestions to me, Jim Halperin, 100 Heritage Plaza, Highland Park Village, Dallas, Texas 75205.

Application for Membership American Numismatic Association
Use Original or Photo-Copy

Check One: **Please Print**

☐ Reg. ☐ Jr. ☐ Assoc. ☐ 5 year ☐ Club ☐ Life Member

Present or former ANA no., if any _____

☐ Mr. ☐ Mrs. ☐ Ms. ☐ Club

Name _____

Street _____

City _____ State _____ Zip _____

Birth Date _____ Occupation _____

ANA Bylaws require the publication of each applicant's name and state.

☐ **Check here if you DO NOT want your name and address forwarded to the ANA Representative in your area.**

☐ **Check here if you would like your name provided to companies with offers we feel may interest you.**

I herewith make application for membership in the American Numismatic Association, subject to the Bylaws of said Association. I also agree to abide by the Code of Ethics adopted by the Association.

Signature of Applicant _____ Date _____

Signature of Proposer _____ Life Member #1306

Signature of Second Proposer
  (optional)_____

Signature of Parent or Guardian_____
  (required for Junior applicant)

Account Number (all digits) ☐ MasterCard ☐ VISA ☐ Check ☐ Money Order

Expiration Date of Card _____

Signature of Cardholder Required_____

Dues

Regular (Adult) – U.S. only . . . .$ 32.00*
Regular (Adult) – All other countries 34.00*
Club – Any country 36.00*
Junior (Under age 18 – no minimum) 11.00
Associate (Child or spouse of regular or life member living at member's address) 4.00
Life (Adult individual) Installment, $40.00 with application,** plus $60.00 per month for 12 months. $750.00
Life (Club) 1,250.00

*First year dues only; subsequent years $6.00 less.
**Includes $10.00 bookkeeping fee, deducted from final payment if made within 90 days of application. Life membership is not effective until full $750.00 is paid.

Foreign applications must be accompanied by U.S. Funds drawn on a U.S. bank.

The Numismatist

Nonmember annual subscription – U.S. only 28.00
Subscription – All other countries 33.00
Send Completed Application to: American Numismatic Association, 818 North Cascade Ave., Colorado Springs, CO 80903-3279

About the Author

Jim Halperin was born in Boston, Massachusetts in 1952, and has been a professional numismatist since 1969, when he opened Jim's Stamp & Coin Shop, in Cochituate, Mass. He attended Harvard College, but took a leave of absence (which so far has turned out to be a permanent one) in 1971, halfway through his sophomore year, to become a full time coin dealer.

In late 1982, Jim Halperin moved to Dallas, Texas, to form a partnership with long time friend and arch-rival, Steve Ivy.

Jim Halperin and Steve Ivy's company, Heritage Capital Corporation, is now possibly the largest and certainly one of the most well respected coin and stamp firms in the world. It's divisions and affiliates include Heritage Rare Coin Galleries, Heritage Coin Wholesale, Heritage Numismatic Auctions, U.S. Rare Coin Exchange, Steve Ivy Philatelic Auctions, U.S. Tangible Investment Corporation and the Numismatic Certification Institute.

Jim is considered to be among the world's foremost experts on U.S. coins and coin grading. His other interests include late 19th and 20th century paintings

Jim Halperin – ANA Life Member #1306

and sculpture, art nouveau glass, comic art, weightlifting and raquetball.

Jim currently lives near Dallas, Texas with his wife, Gayle, a professor of dance. They met in mid-1982 in New York City (appropriately at the Lone Star Cafe). Gayle had been dancing professionally for a modern dance company in New York City, and also taught at Yale University, New Haven, Connecticut. They have been blissfully married since 1984, and Gayle now teaches dance technique at Texas Woman's University.

Jim and Gayle have also set up a foundation based in Dallas to promote the teaching of daily health education courses in public schools.

This book's forerunner, the *N.C.I. Grading Guide* was Jim's first book, although he has written dozens of articles for numismatic publications. Jim hopes to write several other educational numismatic books, and is presently looking for ideas and suggestions of topics for his next book.

Any correspondence should be addressed to:

Jim Halperin
100 Heritage Plaza
Highland Park Village
Dallas, Texas 75205